"A must-have reference book for exec. need to digitize their organizations and leverage data as an actual asset."

—**LEANDRO ANDRADE**, Senior VP, Chief Data & Analytics Officer no Banco de Crédito

"The book data practitioners have been waiting for."

—**NINO LETTERIELLO**, President, DAMA Italia, and CEO and Founder, ENNE Management Consulting

"*Data Juice* trades data and AI hype for practical, real-world examples to inspire leaders and innovators."

—**PAUL DRENNAN**, SVP Chief Commercial & Operations Data Science Officer, The Hartford

"A body of knowledge that should be required reading for boards of directors, executives and industry leaders ... A master class for current and future leaders in the practical applications of data. Highly recommended."

—**ANDREW ANDREWS**, Vice President, DAMA Australia, and Data Governance Lead, Group Risk Information Delivery, ANZ

"*Data Juice* is refreshing! It should be read by both those starting their data journey and those looking to turbo-boost their own initiatives."

—**BARRY PANAYI**, Chief Data & Insight Officer, John Lewis Partnership

"*Data Juice* is a timely, complementary, and empowering follow-up to Laney's breakthrough book, *Infonomics*, and is a must-read for anyone who is serious about understanding data and its value."

—**BENJAMIN WILES**, Chief Data Officer, Clemson University

"If you can't find a story in this book that inspires you to do something amazing with your data assets, then you aren't looking hard enough."

—**CORTNIE ABERCROMBIE**, CEO and Founder, AI Truth

"Doug Laney has done it again! Already established as the go-to source for valuing data assets, he further illustrates that real organizations are getting more value from their data. You will come away energized and inspired."

—**DANETTE MCGILVRAY**, Owner, Granite Falls Consulting, and author of *Executing Data Quality Projects: Ten Steps to Quality Data and Trusted Information*

"After the enormous success of **Infonomics**, Doug knocked it out of the park once again with **Data Juice**. It is an invaluable resource and a must-read for leaders who are motivated but are struggling to extract the "juice" from their data & analytics investments."

—PHANII PYDIMARRI, Senior Director, AI & Analytics Products, Stanley Black & Decker

"An incredible array of commentaries and thought-leadership."

—ROBERT (BOB) S. SEINER, President & Principal, KIK Consulting & Educational Services, and publisher of The Data Administration Newsletter

"This wonderful book inspires by example and shows that data's value is inevitable."

—CHIEF DATA OFFICER, Ministry of Justice and Security, Netherlands

"If I had this book years ago, I could have increased my value driver velocity by 50%. If you want to solidify your success, **Data Juice** should be required reading."

—SALEMA RICE, Global Managing Director, Applied Intelligence, Accenture

"Who says lightning doesn't strike twice? Doug has done it again, proving that his mega-hit **Infonomics** wasn't a lucky accident."

—TIM CARMICHAEL, Chief Data Officer, Chalhoub Group

"This book is about actual results, not speculation, and sprinkled with bits of Doug's humor to lighten it up."

—TOM AUSTIN, CEO, The Analyst Syndicate

"**Data Juice** is your inspirational guide on how to digitally transform your organization and finally realize the value of data. An absolute must-have for all CEOs, CDOs, and other leaders responsible for helping their organizations become more data-driven and data-savvy."

—VINCENT YATES, Chief Data Officer, Credera

"A great help for building an appealing story of why data matters in the future of every company."

—ALICE VASKOVA, Director of Enterprise Analytics Demand & Capability, Philip Morris International

"Hands-down one of the most useful resources on how organizations are extracting value from their data assets globally. A masterful job of weaving together a comprehensive set of real-world examples with expert insights that take the reader beyond the "sugar high" of hype. Essential reading for business leaders. Doug's storytelling, experience, and expert insights made this book tough to put down."

—ALOIS NYAMAREBVU, CEO, Data Fluent Africa

"The timing of Doug's book is perfect. Leaders are not looking for hypothetical or abstract examples. Real-world examples are what they're looking for to help increase data literacy."

—JAMES ESELGROTH, Director, Data & Analytics, RIVA Solutions

"*Data Juice* is an energetic and powerful reminder to skeptical executives who still doubt valuing data is a competitive advantage."

—LIONEL LOPEZ, Chief Data Officer, National Bank of Canada

"A treasure trove of high-value examples and practical advice, *Data Juice* is a must-read for business leaders."

—OMRI KOHL, Co-Founder & CEO, Pyramid Analytics

"Written by the greatest author on data monetization, Doug Laney, *Data Juice* has delivered an exciting follow up to his book on Infonomics and one that will become required reading for all who are on the path to success for their business. This book is an exciting opportunity to learn from the top consultants, advisors, practitioners, leaders, and futurists on how businesses became leading data innovators."

—ROBERT LUTTON, VP, Sandhill Consultants, and Program Director, MIT CDOIQ Symposium

"A must-read for any data strategist. You are guaranteed to find inspiration in this book, no matter your background and experience."

—RUBEN SARDARYAN, CEO & Founder, Infocratic

"This is the finest collection of real-world stories and an invaluable resource. I see myself referring to this book every time I am thinking about the new possibilities of data and analytics."

—SHASHANK GARG, Co-Founder & CEO, InfoCepts

"The monetization of data is the most pressing issue for today's C-suite leader. Doug's global experience helping companies go beyond the "new oil" is brought to life in real-world examples of value creation, revenue, and profits."

—**STEVE WANNAMAKER**, Publisher and CEO, Chief Data Officer Magazine

"The Father of Infonomics brings insights to life in his uniquely engaging style. This book is required reading for CEOs, CFOs, private equity professionals, CDOs, and literally anybody looking to derive quantifiable value from data."

—**SUNIL SOARES**, Co-Founder & CEO, YourDataConnect

"Like sitting around the table with an expert set of data and business leaders sharing their stories and experiences . . . Inspiration for all leaders."

—**TINA ROSARIO**, Chief Data Officer, Europe, SAP

"I highly recommend this authentic and unique book . . . there isn't another like it. Doug Laney is a remarkable writer and thought leader."

—**WALID EL ABED**, Founder and CEO, Global Data Excellence

"Like getting an accelerated, data-focused MBA . . . *Data Juice* deserves an easy-to-reach location on every business professional's and executive's bookshelf!"

—**ANTHONY ALGMIN**, Convergence Platform Program Lead, AbbVie, and Founder and CEO, Algmin Data Leadership

"Will help accelerate your understanding and inspire new ideas on how to utilize data."

—**COREY FERENGUL**, Chief Executive Officer at Yello.co

"There's gold in them thar hills! Or at least there is locked away in data silos. *Data Juice* is very useful to those charged with deciding on the best use-cases for data-related initiatives."

—**DAVID FINLAY**, Medical Device Industry Master Data Consultant, Data Driven Associates

"A must-read for executives who seek what management consultants advise, without hiring the management consultant."

—**NAEEM HASHMI**, Digital Health Solutions Strategic Advisor, Boston Scientific

"Definitively, this will be the reference book for any data and analytics professional for many years to come."

—**SANDRO DENEGRI**, Chief Data Officer—Head of Data, Analytics & CRM, Mibanco

"An essential read for senior executives, especially those who are directly responsible for generating value from their organizations' data assets. This book draws in the reader and keeps them engaged."

—VISHAL CHAUDHRY, Chief Data Officer, Washington State Health Care Authority

"An invaluable trove of knowledge, best practices across the field of data science. A must-read for anyone looking to make sense of the Digital Age."

—HANNS-CHRISTIAN HANEBECK, Founder & CEO, Truckl

"*Data Juice* is the impeccable collection of diversified use-cases for every business or data leader. A must-read for every business transformation leader or data leader who aspires to capitalize data and treat data as an asset."

—IMAD SYED, CEO and Chief Information Officer, PiLog Group

"Just as *Infonomics* was groundbreaking, *Data Juice* is a valuable resource for every data professional. Everyone should have *Data Juice* on their desk."

—MORGAN TEMPLAR, Vice President, Information Management, Highmark Health

"A great resource to help educate your peers and ideate transformation ideas for your own organization."

—NICOLAS AVERSENG, Founder & CEO, YOOI

"*Data Juice* is an essential book to cut through the noise around all things data."

—MATHIEU GUERVILLE, Associate Director, New Ventures, CCC Intelligent Solutions

"Will help data management professionals start thinking more about business results and be more effective partners with business executives."

—RICHARD HOWEY, Founder and CEO, Technoscan Systems

DATA
JUICE

-Doug Lang

DATA JUICE

101 Stories of How Organizations Are Squeezing Value from Available Data Assets

featuring commentaries by dozens of the world's top thought leaders and practitioners

Douglas B. Laney

Best-selling author of *Infonomics*

To Susan and Ethan

*Ah, the stories our little family has
that will never be written!* 😊

TABLE OF CONTENTS

VALUE DRIVER INDEX

VALUE DRIVER	STORY NUMBERS
Revenue	2, 10, 11, 14, 18, 19, 21, 25, 32, 33, 34, 36, 52, 55, 83
Growth	4, 8, 9, 10, 11, 14, 15, 16, 25, 31, 34, 35, 42, 44, 60, 66, 67, 70, 73, 75, 76, 77, 80, 82, 83, 88, 90, 93, 96, 101
Experience	3, 6, 9, 15, 17, 21, 24, 29, 33, 38, 41, 43, 45, 47, 48, 49, 50, 56, 58, 64, 68, 69, 75, 78, 84, 86, 87, 94, 96, 97, 99, 100
Retention	14, 15, 22, 32, 35, 39, 40, 44, 46, 50, 60, 66, 67, 69, 70, 73, 86, 90, 91, 92, 93, 95, 96, 98, 101
Quality	6, 7, 13, 16, 27, 28, 53, 57, 59, 78, 88, 100
Completeness	28, 52, 59, 62, 71, 74, 89, 99
Stability	26, 43, 53, 63, 68, 86
Efficiency	1, 5, 7, 12, 13, 16, 18, 20, 21, 22, 23, 27, 30, 31, 33, 37, 39, 42, 46, 49, 51, 53, 56, 57, 58, 59, 61, 62, 63, 65, 71, 74, 81, 82, 85, 87, 88, 90, 91, 93, 94, 95, 97, 98, 100
Costs	1, 5, 7, 8, 12, 13, 18, 20, 26, 27, 28, 30, 34, 36, 38, 39, 45, 46, 48, 49, 51, 53, 55, 57, 58, 64, 74, 78, 90, 93, 98
Simplicity	12, 23, 29, 31, 51, 58, 59, 65, 72, 79, 81, 85, 95
Reputation	4, 29, 30, 37, 40, 41, 47, 49, 54, 63, 82, 84, 87, 89, 92, 100
Compliance	4, 19, 23, 24, 26, 37, 38, 40, 47, 54, 58, 68, 72, 76, 84, 89, 92, 97
Risk	46, 49, 51, 52, 53, 54, 57, 59, 64, 68, 72, 75, 78, 86, 92
Agility	3, 10, 11, 25, 29, 32, 36, 53, 55, 61, 64, 71, 74, 78, 79, 81, 82, 83, 87, 88, 95, 96, 101
Differentiation	2, 6, 9, 15, 17, 19, 24, 35, 41, 42, 43, 45, 48, 50, 52, 56, 60, 61, 62, 65, 66, 67, 69, 70, 72, 73, 75, 76, 77, 80, 82, 89, 91, 92, 95, 99
Margin	20, 27, 28, 42, 44, 62, 64, 77, 78, 80, 81, 85, 88, 90, 93, 94, 97

ACKNOWLEDGMENTS

My wife chided me that if I ever wrote another book, it would have to be titled, "How I Used Big Data to Find My Next Wife." If you've ever written a book before or taken on a similarly challenging and time-consuming endeavor, you'll completely understand. So, first of all, I would like to acknowledge Susan for her support and encouragement. Second, I'd like to thank all the businesses and other organizations for sharing their stories to help inspire others, and to all the experts who contributed analyses—in effect to everyone who pretty much wrote this book for me!

Additionally, I would like to extend my gratitude to the management team at West Monroe for supporting this project, especially Greg Layok, and our Data Engineering and Analytics practice partners, Matt Rager, Penny Wand, and Brad Ptasienski. And also to the West Monroe marketing team, in particular Casey Foss, Christina Galoozis, Lindsay Michelini, and Shira Cohen.

Many thanks also to the following individuals and organizations:

- Scott Watson, Karan Dhawal, Heide Laz, Mosiur Rahman, Farwa Haider, and Paul Sutliff who actively supported the effort by researching, editing and tagging stories, and otherwise assisting with organizing the effort

- The 1106 Design Team for their editing, layout, and self-publishing support

- Brad Laney at Anatomy Marketing for the cover design and other branding goodies

Finally, I would like to acknowledge some other special folks who, while not involved directly, have continued to support and inspire me along the way, including Stan Rosenthal; James Price; John Ladley; Tom Redman; Chris Adamson at TDWI; Tony Shaw at Dataversity; David Ulcine and David Steier at Carnegie Mellon; Brooke Elliot, Gary Hecht and all my students the past few years at the University of Illinois Gies College of Business; Rich Wang, Robert Lutton and the entire MIT CDOIQ Symposium staff; John Bottega, Brian McConnell and everyone at the Enterprise Data Management Council; various DAMA chapter officers; Martin Giles at Forbes; Steve Wannamaker at CDO Magazine; Ranjana Young; Jon Hahn; Neil Raden; Gokula Mishra; Scott Taylor; Bill Schmarzo; Jimmy & Sylvia Schwarzkopf and Einat Shimoni at STKI; Herman Heyns; all my collaborators with the World Economic Forum, the Enterprise Data Management Council; and the friends and former colleagues at Gartner who prodded me into publishing these stories.

INTRODUCTION

Data monetization. Digitalization. Data-driven. Or just Analytics or Business Intelligence.

However we care to refer to the concept this year or next it's ultimately about creating new sources of value from data, directly or indirectly.

As one chief data officer told me, "Data and analytics success stories are a dime-a-dozen, but what's really lacking are use cases with actual, hard benefits." Other business and data executives have echoed the same sentiment, some lamenting how most vendor stories are fluff with no actual measured value, others chastising the analyst and consulting communities for fabricating use cases for illustrative purposes. Personally, if someone can't tell me the benefits of their data or analytics implementation beyond, "It's faster!," "There are lots of users!," or even "We can do X better" with no indication of amplitude, then I'm not particularly interested. Nor should you be.

In my previous book, *Infonomics: How to Monetize, Manage, and Measure Information as an Asset for Competitive Advantage,* I sprinkled dozens of real-world, high-value examples throughout. But clients and colleagues have practically begged more—an actual compilation of practicable ideas to inspire them, or to shame their management into doing more with the organization's data.

As a result, over the past several years I set about to compile several hundred actual stories with certain criteria: 1) from a named, not anonymous, organization, 2) verifiable, 3) of sufficient detail, and 4) with significant measurable economic or societal benefits. This is what you'll find in the pages that follow, not marketing fodder, hype, nor vendor shilling. Yes, specific vendors and their wares often are mentioned, but this is not the point. Technologies come and go, but good ideas on how to deploy data have greater longevity.

True, the art of the possible with data goes well beyond many of these stories—leveraging AI, digital twins, or the promise of blockchain and quantum computing. Yet these examples for the most part are approachable, adaptable and doable for almost any organization. Speaking of which, you will find that these stories focus on the *what* not the *how*. They are meant to aid you and your team to establish or expand your vision for the possibilities of data, not to lay out an actual implementation plan.

But wait, that's not all...

Expert Analyses

As inspirational as these stories are by themselves, I wanted them to hit-home even better by having each one include a unique analysis and commentary by one of dozens of experts—some of the world's top data and analytics consultants, advisors, practitioners, leaders and futurists. These experts have offered their thoughts on:

- What stood out to them about each story

- What particular challenges have they have experienced with this kind of solution and how have they been overcome

- How the solution could be adapted to other industries, and

- Recommendations on how to build upon or expand each implementation.

I am truly honored to know and have learned from each of these thought leaders over the course of my career and am indebted to them for their contributions to this project. And now you can learn from them too.

And yet there's more . . .

Industry, Location, Value Indices and #Hashtags

The book also contains several different indices to the stories, based on their industry, location, and value drivers. Clients often ask me, "What are others in our market or in our country doing with data?" My flippant response usually is, "Why do you want to be in second or third place?" Why not adopt and adapt ideas from others outside your sector or locale to be the first one to do so? Still, in an appeal to the fast-followers and laggards, I have included these indices.

The index I believe most valuable, no surprise, is the value index. Each story has been assigned one or more value drivers corresponding to the type of benefits realized. In addition to the value index, each story is accompanied by a Value Compass like the one below so you can quickly identify what outcomes were achieved.

FIGURE 1: Value Compass

And for those with an electronic copy of the book, each story is preceded by a set of searchable hashtags corresponding to the key concepts within, including geography and industry. #yourewelcome

A Meta Analysis

In addition to the individual expert analyses provided for each use case, you may also notice certain patterns emerge across the spectrum of stories. These meta tendencies in-and-of themselves are really quite instructive, e.g.:

- An organization doesn't have to be big to leverage big data, and an organization doesn't have to have big data to do big things with it.

- Many organizations make use of data beyond their own four walls, including syndicated data, open data, social media, web content, or data from partners.

- Many organizations find incredibly valuable uses for data they've collected, used for a single purpose, and forgotten about or archived, i.e., their "dark data."

- Many stories involve the use and mining of unstructured content, not just structured customer or transaction data.

- Most use cases cite multiple benefits, sometimes even multiple measured benefits.

- High value implementations do not necessarily require enterprise-wide data warehouses or data lakes, but rather are targeted and vocational, focusing on a single problem or opportunity with a limited set of data.

- Most use cases focus on improving revenue or margin, but the cleverest ones and those with the most ancillary benefits tend to focus on other drivers like customer experience or agility.

- Almost none of the examples involve hindsight-oriented dashboards or scorecards. Real value comes from diagnostic, predictive and prescriptive solutions—or new business models altogether.

- Most implementations involve a degree of integration, not just data integration, but integrating the analytic output or data streams directly into business processes or operational systems. Directing analytics at eyeballs is so very last century and does not generate much ROIA (return on information assets).

- Most stories are driven by business leaders, not IT leaders.

- Productizing and licensing data, creating digital solutions, and using data as a form of collateral are emerging forms of data monetization that are fast introducing entirely new value streams for businesses.

Also, I have noticed through my research and consulting that certain kinds of data are more monetizable than other data. When working with clients on monetization initiatives, I typically start with identifying data with as many of these eight monetizable characteristics as possible:

1. Data that originates with your organization or for which you have some claim of provenance and control

2. Data that is proprietary in nature in that others do not have it or data like it

3. Data that is of a general or accepted context, rather than data that may not be particularly meaningful outside your organization or industry

4. Data that is secure. If it is easily accessed or hacked can result in a black market for it which may cannibalize your own efforts to monetize it

5. Data that is not restricted in the way you are able to collect or deploy it (E.g., Privacy regulations may be an inhibitor, but not entirely preventative if you're clever enough.)

6. Data that is sufficiently accurate and precise for the intended purpose(s)

7. Data that is complete, in that it represents a significant slice of the known universe of such activities or entities, and for which any given record is complete (e.g., without missing fields)

8. Data that is and will be available for the foreseeable future, or for which alternatives are available inside your organization

Within these data monetizable sources identified, then you can dig deeper to identify what Rockwell Automation's enterprise data leader, Karan Dhawal, refers to as "monetizable data elements" (MDEs).

Data Monetization Patterns

As I discussed in *Infonomics*, monetizing data can take a variety of forms. Several patterns have emerged when assessing the hundreds of stories I have collected. Data monetization isn't just about selling data. More broadly and concisely I define data monetization as: *generating new, measurable value streams from available data assets.* This definition opens up a whole world of possibilities, including: using available data that's not necessarily your own as discussed above, and generating a wide variety of economic or societal benefits—albeit ones that can be quantified.

Data monetization falls into two broad categories: Indirect Data Monetization and Direct Data Monetization. Indirect data monetization involves solutions focused more so on internal business processes that generate measurable returns, while direct data monetization involves externalizing data in return for some type of commercial consideration. See Figure 2.

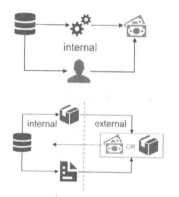

INDIRECT DATA MONETIZATION
- Improving process performance or effectiveness
- Reducing risk / improving compliance
- Developing new products or markets
- Building and solidifying partner relationships
- Assetizing data via special corporate structures
- Publishing branded indices to promote data products/services

DIRECT DATA MONETIZATION
- Bartering/trading with data for non-cash commercial considerations
- Enhancing products or services with data
- Licensing raw data through brokers or data markets
- Selling insights, analyses and reports
- "Inverted" data monetization via referral arrangements
- Collateralizing data to securitize loans

FIGURE 2: Data Monetization Methods

Productizing and Packaging Data

But why get fixated on just one data monetization method? Data is what economists would call a non-rivalrous, non-depleting, progenitive resource—one that can be used multiple ways simultaneously, doesn't get "used-up" when consumed, and that typically generates more data when it's used. No, data absolutely is *not* "the new oil." Oil doesn't have any of these incredible economic characteristics. And winning businesses are the ones taking full advantage of data's unique qualities. In fact, according to infonomics research I performed, businesses demonstrating data-savvy behavior have nearly a 200% greater market-to-book value than the market average, and for data product companies (i.e. those that primarily sell data or data derivatives) this ratio is 300% higher. There's no doubt that investors positively love data-driven companies.

Because of these unique aspects of data, it can be packaged in numerous ways. (See Figure 3.) These range from publishing raw data, to rolling it up in to analyses, to creating custom and integration solutions. Just as with other raw materials, however, the more you process them the more expensive and exclusive they become. Consider wheat. Wheat itself is quite the commodity—relatively inexpensive but with a massive global demand. Then it can be processed into different kinds of flour with specific but still a wide range of uses, then into breads which are more expensive and with a lesser range of uses, and finally integrated with other resources into sandwiches or cakes with more premium price tags and smaller, more localized markets.

FIGURE 3: Data Packaging Options

Similarly, each subsequent step of processing your available data assets can result in them delivering more specific and greater value, yet to a smaller market (user base).

Your Data Monetization Journey

Finally, I'll address the "how." Although data may have incredible characteristics that other resources and assets like physical materials, financial assets, human capital, and even other intangible asset do not, we need not consider it anomalous when it comes to data monetization initiatives. Instead, I recommend borrowing from well-honed product management approaches to lay out your data monetization function. (See figure

Central to treating data as an asset, data monetization should align with familiar research and development (R&D) and product management/marketing approaches. Not to oversimplify the many challenges and activities involved in monetizing data, certain basic concepts will reap significant rewards if executed well.

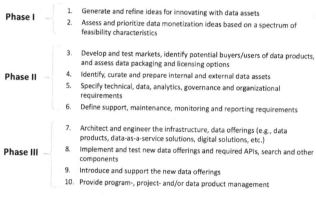

Phase I
1. Generate and refine ideas for innovating with data assets
2. Assess and prioritize data monetization ideas based on a spectrum of feasibility characteristics

Phase II
3. Develop and test markets, identify potential buyers/users of data products, and assess data packaging and licensing options
4. Identify, curate and prepare internal and external data assets
5. Specify technical, data, analytics, governance and organizational requirements
6. Define support, maintenance, monitoring and reporting requirements

Phase III
7. Architect and engineer the infrastructure, data offerings (e.g., data products, data-as-a-service solutions, digital solutions, etc.)
8. Implement and test new data offerings and required APIs, search and other components
9. Introduce and support the new data offerings
10. Provide program-, project- and/or data product management

FIGURE 4: Data Monetization Roadmap

The details, specific methods and tools behind each of these phases and steps is beyond the scope of this book, but available via the courses and workshops I teach and the services my colleagues at West Monroe and I provide.

Overcoming The Myths and Roadblocks

Along the road to conceiving and creating new data-driven value streams for your organization, you will invariably bump up against any number of data monetization myths and potential showstoppers. Be very prepared for them, or work with someone who can help your organization get better educated and prepared via instruction and workshops, a data literacy program, and/or a change management initiative.

Many of the myths about data monetization persist today, and will continue to do so until business leaders, legal counsels, CFOs and controllers, company executives and boards become better aware and educated on the possibilities and realities of data.

MYTH	REALITY
Data must be sold to be monetized.	Data can be used indirectly or internally to generate measurable economic benefits.
Data monetization requires an exchange of cash.	Data can be exchanged with others for goods, services or favorable commercial terms.
Data monetization only involves your own data.	Integrating others' data, even freely available data sources, with your own improves its utility and value. You can even collect and productize freely available data itself.
One can only monetize raw data.	Data can be packaged and productized in a wide variety of ways.
Only data that's used has any value.	This is inconsistent with how other assets are valued. Simply having and holding data can have certain economic benefits.
One must be in the data business to monetize information.	At least 30% of non-data-product organizations are monetizing their data today.
Our data is specific to us and no value to others.	Your partners and suppliers, especially, would beg to differ.
It's best for us just to share our information with our suppliers and partners.	This is a slippery slope that becomes more expensive than its worth. Set the bar at what they get for free versus what you offer for a premium. And consider your extended business ecosystem, e.g. your partner's suppliers, or customers' partners.
Due to privacy regulations, we cannot monetize our customer data.	You can't sell or even share your customer data with others, but you can sell others' offerings to your customers for a referral fee or commission. (Think: Facebook)

Even once you've moved your organization beyond these myths, you'll still find a range or roadblocks along your journey that must be moved or navigated around, including:

- Core business priorities making data monetization a low(er) priority

- Mental blocks due to data not (yet) being a recognized asset because of archaic accounting standards

- Legal, regulatory, or ethical roadblocks (perceived and real)

- Already giving away data for free

- Insufficient foundational capabilities such as data integration, masterdata management, analytics, storage/computing capacity

- Insufficient data quality (accuracy, completeness, timeliness, integrity, etc.)

- No culture of R&D, especially with data

- Lack of organizational experience and skills

Final Thought

Economists have long touted the four factors of production as the key components of industry. They are: Land, Labor, Capital, and Entrepreneurship. I contend that not only does (should) data qualify as an actual balance sheet asset, but that it has ascended to become a fifth factor of production. With this book in hand, it's time for you and your organization to get way more productive with data. I look forward to learning about the new data-driven value streams you create for your business, and perhaps including them in a subsequent version of this book or an upcoming article.

1. PREDICTIVE ANALYTICS CAN BE COOL

#hotel #hospitality #usa #northamerica #energy
#utilities #kaizen #predictive #reporting #equipment
#savings #expense #energysavings #HVAC
#environment #construction #building #property

Millennium Partners LLC specializes in the building and management of luxury residential and commercial properties in major cities. Each property Millennium Partners creates is unique in character and design–luxurious residential environments with the perfect balance of location and amenities where residents can work and immerse in distinctive city experiences.

Founded in 1992, Millennium Partners has headquarters in New York and currently employs 500 individuals. The company has completed major mixed-use developments in New York, Boston, Washington DC, San Francisco, and Miami at a cost of over $4 billion. Millennium Partners owns and operates The Offices, a 10-story class "A" office building located at Four Seasons Hotel and Tower Miami. They planned to retrofit the building's HVAC (heating, ventilation, and air conditioning) in keeping with system control and energy efficiency improvements. South Florida Controls was called in to make a study of the potential energy savings that can be generated from implementing the building system renovation.

South Florida Controls demonstrated that the project will not just pay for itself through future energy cost savings, but also generate a healthy return on investment. It used CopperTree Analytics' CopperCube to extract current and historical trend logs from the building automation system. To investigate the building and establish a baseline, trend logs were then processed by CopperTree's Kaizen, an analytics engine and logic builder. The use of these tools enabled them to view energy trends in the building and customizable reports gave them the ability to pinpoint which equipment and systems could deliver the most energy-savings impact. It also enabled them to build a model predicting return on investment of the renovation through the energy cost savings to be realized.

Following implementation, the building owners and operators have seen a reduction in their electrical energy consumption of 64% per month. As it turned out, the projected savings from the study was within 1% of the actual values that were projected: nearly $60,000 per year in electricity savings. With the proven reliability of the tools used in the project, South Florida Controls and Millennium Partners now have an established solution they can use to project the savings and ROI on future renovations in this and other buildings in their portfolio.

Expert Analysis by Gokula Mishra

VP of Data Science at Direct Supply

In this use case, certainly predictive analytics was very beneficial in creating savings in energy cost, and recently is being looked at by many large real estate property owners and managers. Some of the challenges to keep in mind:

- *Do factor in weather data into predictive analytics, it can save a lot of hassles if predictive maintenance is not accurate and weather forecast was not included.*

- *Also advise strongly to include MTBF (Mean Time Between Failure) data from original manufacturer of machines to prevent unnecessary maintenance that may not be able to prevent the failure of the machines or might require frequent repairs, may be it's time to replace the machine.*

Predictive analytics can be very beneficial for the manufacturer of the machine—if the prediction can save on maintenance, maybe one can think about offering the service rather than sell the product—such as temperature-as-a-service or tire-mile as-a-service.

2. Analytics is the Future of Retail

#ecommerce #mcommerce #retail #analytics
#ai #india #asia #predictive #customer
#loyalty #advancedanalytics

E-Commerce is a complicated business. It may look simple from the perspective of buyers, whose activities include browsing through thousands of items, adding chosen products to their shopping cart, paying via credit card or other payment options, and waiting for their goods to be delivered at their doorstep.

For online business owners, on the other hand, it's a whole different story altogether. Many different elements must be connected and integrated to make the operations run smoothly, seamlessly, and successfully. Take Future Group, India's leading conglomerate, for example. On a typical day, Future Group receives over 2 million online customers in their stores and digital platforms. Imagine how the company manages, interacts, and nurtures this volume of customers daily. Therefore, Future Group partnered with Manthan, a US-based company specializing in analytics and AI solutions. Future Group wanted to grow its business and

4

explore more opportunities in the Indian retail markets and stores and using analytics tools and big data was the solution they came up with.

For Future Retail, one of the multiple entities of Future Group, acquiring analytical abilities enables them to identify customer opportunities at a deeper and more granular level. Analytics data from Manthan gives them the flexibility to connect to their customers in real-time, with any product, on any channel, and at any store.

Manthan provides data-driven business applications and advanced analytics solutions to more than 200 clients across the globe, enabling them to reach a wider audience and increase market share in their respective industries. On average, Manthan's analytics tools can track and monitor over 10 million customer transactions every month, from more than 3,000 suppliers and over 13,000 product brands and 3,000 suppliers. The provided data and analytics give Future Group valuable, precise, and real-time actionable information in its more than 370 stores across 166 Indian cities.

As a result, Future Group companies and stores can tailor their offerings, product inventory, marketing promotions, advertising messages, store engagement campaigns to the shopping behavior of their customers. They are also able to track the activities of 30 million loyalty program customers and provide them with personalized offers. Example Monetized data element: Customer Age

Through Manthan's analytics-driven solutions, Future Group has improved its customer targeting and personalized messaging across a multitude of channels and has adapted rapid predictive modeling for specific strategic and tactical business objectives.

Expert Analysis by Andrew Sohn,

Data and Analytics consultant and former
Chief Data and Analytics Officer

Future Retail took two crucial actions that helped them generate business value quickly. The first is they partnered with a company that already had a proven product instead of building their own system. They may want to build proprietary capabilities in the future, but they would put themselves at a competitive disadvantage if they started with that path. In online marketplaces, speed to delivery is critical.

The other thing they did is join a data ecosystem. Although many companies are initially resistant to contributing their data to an exchange, the value of the data they receive back in return is significant. Being able to know more about their customers, and reach additional target customers, is the key to growth.

Companies in similar situations need to consider what data they have and what additional data they need. It's not enough to collect data; you must plan what you want to do with the data and how to manage it. It is also necessary to plan for delivering and using the data at the point of decision, such as during a real-time web shopping session or checkout. If you can't deliver a real-time call to action with up-to-date data, you'll be squandering much of the investment value in analytics.

3: National Library's Search Index Goes on a Data Diet

#japan #asia #digitalarchive #apache #hadoop #dataprocessing #seo #recommendation #document #indexing #search #selfservice

Located in Chiyoda City in Tokyo, the National Diet Library (NDL) collects, stores, and preserves both written materials and digital information from Japan and other countries worldwide, serving as a repository of knowledge, language, and culture. As part of Japan's National Diet, the Library assists in the activities of the country's legislature and provides library services to Japan's judicial and administrative entities, as well as the Japanese citizens.

The NDL, as a national library, is responsible for acquiring and preserving, not only traditional books and paper materials but also digital contents, making them accessible for everyone anytime and anywhere. To be able to achieve this, the need for creating a digital archive became necessary. The objective of NDL's digital archive will help store, manage, and process huge volumes of data, and efficiently aggregate search results into a semantically significant group.

The development of the NDL Search started with an open-source software called the Apache Hadoop, which was used to speed up full-text search indexing and automatic bibliographic grouping. The system used more than 30 Hadoop nodes and processed data volume at around 5TB, which is equivalent to tens of millions of items.

By taking advantage of online tools and technology, the National Diet Library was able to capture and manage a huge volume of data, create a search index from all its documents, and reduce the time for manual searching of materials and information. These results do not only enable library users and readers to access information more efficiently; more importantly, they also create new knowledge by reusing existing information and building a usable knowledge infrastructure.

Expert Analysis by Howard Dresner,
Founder and Chief Research Officer,
Dresner Advisory Services

It's laudable that the National Diet Library has successfully created a digital archive, with indexing and search capabilities. This alone will save countless amounts of time for researchers.

However, the value of creating massive online volumes of data goes beyond that feat. The greater value is the ability to distill large sets of data down to meaningful essence. Any organization with large sets of data, like NDL, ought to expand access using alternative data structures such as graph to make exploration of data more fluid. Additionally, large sets of data also lend themselves to the use of machine learning (e.g., clustering, classification) to guide users to the most significant bits of information more readily. Additionally, organizations should capture usage metadata so that over time they can highlight the most popular paths through the data by other users. And, finally, governance processes and standards will be important to maintaining and increasing the value of the data and insights over time.

4: BIG DATA IS JUST THE TICKET FOR REDUCING FRAUD

#usa #northamerica #marketplace #ecommerce #analytics #datawarehouse #partitioning #recommendation #reporting #customer

StubHub, an eBay company and one of the world's largest ticket marketplaces, enables web users to buy and sell different types of tickets to various sports and entertainment events worldwide. It serves as an online hub where consumers and fans can buy or sell their tickets fast, safely, and conveniently.

Managing global customers and monitoring millions of transactions coming from over 25 different data sources, the platform's biggest issues included daily churns, fraudulent activities, customer-related concerns, and more. Efficient processing and analysis of volumes of big data were also a critical challenge for the company.

To help address these problems, StubHub taps into big data to acquire valuable insights about their customers' ticket buying patterns and behaviors. It implemented a single data warehouse to store and process information on millions of customers from multiple data sources, resulting in the following benefits:

- Delivering insight about churn prediction, fraud notification and alerts, and product recommendations.

- Enabling faster, smarter, and more efficient data analysis of customer transactions and online shopping behaviors.

- Providing quick access to customer-related data, including ticket purchase history, patterns, and demographics, and exploring this data to build deploy and multiple data-mining models, create predictions, and improve StubHub's responsiveness. Enabling calculation of 180 million customers' lifetime value compared to just 20,000 values at a time previously possible.

- Reducing fraud issues by up to 90%

Through these innovations that use the power of big data and analytics, StubHub continues to grow and expand in the online sports, concert, theater, and other live-entertainment events ticket marketplace, serving millions of customers worldwide.

Expert Analysis by Dr. James Short,

Director of the Center for Large Scale Data Systems Research (CLDS) at the San Diego Supercomputer Center, University of California San Diego.

StubHub's evolution from data warehouse to the operating platform for the world's largest ticket market shows what can be accomplished in building out a modern, real-time data analytics platform: market leadership, business return on investment, customer knowledge, and predictive modeling about where to go next. In real-time platform development, it's what is under the hood that counts. The StubHub story shows the importance of starting with scale—a data systems infrastructure that will scale as the business pressure-tests it.

Going forward, StubHub's business systems will need to support the full range of analytics use cases, from self-service visualization and exploration to guided analytics apps and dashboards, custom and embedded analytics, mobile analytics, and reporting for its business ecosystem partners and their customers. Starting with scale and sustaining investment and strategy intent will enable StubHub to grow its platform across other live-entertainment ticket marketplaces, leveraging its real time capabilities.

5: WHEN IOT MEANS INTERNET OF TRUCKS

#usa #northamerica #manufacturing #industry #datawarehouse #iot
#telematics #machinelearning #diagnostic #alerting #customer

Navistar International Corporation is a leading vehicle manufacturer based in Lisle, Illinois USA. It specializes in commercial trucks, buses, defense vehicles, and proprietary diesel
engines. International and IC Bus are two of its well-known brands
for its trucks and buses. The company operates through its network
of more than 1,000 dealer outlets and dealers in the US, Canada,
Brazil, Mexico, and more than 60 other countries.

Navistar always has put a focus on improving the uptime of its
trucks and achieving zero downtime due to unplanned maintenance.
In the past, it had to rely on vehicle maintenance schedules based on
miles traveled or the time since a vehicle's last service appointment.
In worst cases, repair had to be done when vehicle eventually breaks
down. This was considered rudimentary and an ineffective method
for maximizing fleet performance and accounted for a large share
of total vehicle owner costs. Breakdowns typically cause a loss in
revenue of up to $1,000 per day.

The traditional data warehouses and the legacy systems Navistar previously used to support the collection, processing, and analysis of high-volume telematics data could not cope with its real-time need to predict maintenance requirements.

Navistar established an IoT-enabled remote diagnostics platform to address its needs. It used OnCommand Connection, on Cloudera Enterprise with SDX. The platform can handle over 70 telematics and sensor data feeds coming from more than 375,000 connected vehicles. These feeds include information on engine performance, truck speed, acceleration, brake wear, and coolant temperature. The new system will then correlate this data with other Navistar and third-party data sources, which include geolocation, meteorological, traffic, vehicle usage, historical warranty, and parts inventory information.

Currently, the platform stores over 60 terabytes of data. It utilizes the results of the learning from machine evaluation of billions of rows of data from connected vehicles and advanced analytics to quickly detect engine problems and predict maintenance requirements.

With the aid of OnCommand Connection, Navistar has helped fleet and vehicle owners to achieve significant reductions in maintenance costs—up to 40%. One Navistar customer has reported its vehicles' maintenance-cost-per-mile has been slashed from $0.12-$0.15 to less than $0.03.

Navistar can also enable fleet and vehicle owners to monitor truck health and performance from smartphones or tablets now, enabling them to prioritize needed repairs and maintenance service.

Expert Analysis by Laura Sebastian-Coleman,

DQ Lead at Aetna, a CVS Health Company

This is a great example of how a technology like diagnostic sensors benefits everyone involved in the shipping process: Navistar, fleet and vehicle owners, drivers, and businesses who rely on efficient delivery of goods. Downtime, breakdowns, and unplanned maintenance are reduced, drivers are safer, and there is a more predictable process with fewer delays. Transportation logistics are all about efficiency, so the ability to proactively prevent delays is a big win. It does not take much imagination to envision an approach like this being applied to public transportation, as well as to private vehicles.

The concept could readily be applied to almost any kind of machinery that requires regular maintenance. It also seems like an optimal application for machine learning since the maintenance process itself can provide feedback about the accuracy of the predictions and thus be used to improve the analytics.

6: Package Delivery Company UPS its Fuel Efficiency

#global #worldwide #logistics #transportation
#telemetrics #chatbots #AI #monitoring #prescriptive

UPS is the world's largest package delivery company. It is a global leader in logistics, offering a broad range of solutions including transporting packages and freight and facilitating international trade. A multi-billion-dollar global corporation, Through its services, it connects 220 nations and territories across roads, rails, air, and ocean. Its more than a century of operation reflects its "Customer first, People led, Innovation driven" philosophy and a commitment to quality service and environmental sustainability.

UPS uses a wide variety of technologies to improve its flexibility, capability, and efficiency. Among the major challenges UPS has is to use the data it collects to boost efficiency and dynamically optimize delivery routes of drivers for reduced fuel consumption and CO2 emissions and faster package delivery.

UPS currently utilizes a fleet management system called ORION (On-road Integrated Optimization and Navigation), which uses telematics and advanced algorithms to create optimal routes for delivery drivers. With ORION, drivers leave the facility having optimized delivery routes. The system dynamically optimizes the routes as their activity progresses and takes into consideration changing road conditions and commitments in real-time.

The UPS IT Team continuously works on other initiatives for a smart logistics network to improve decision making across package delivery networks. It is now into the development of a chatbot that features AI capability to help customers search for information about their packages.

Since ORION's initial deployment, it has saved UPS about 100 million miles and 10 million gallons of fuel per year. This translates into 100,000 metric tons of reduced CO_2 emissions. The latest enhancements UPS is embarking on will significantly improve upon those results.

Expert Analysis by Tom Davenport,

Distinguished Professor of IT and Management, Babson College Visiting Professor, Oxford University Saïd Business School Senior Advisor, Deloitte Analytics and AI Practice Digital Fellow, MIT Initiative on the Digital Economy

ORION is a notable achievement in analytics and data science for multiple reasons. First, it is one of the largest and most expensive projects of this type. I estimated that it cost between $400 and $500 million, and my UPS contacts suggested that was an accurate estimate. Of course, the very large annual savings in fuel and labor costs make it worth such a substantial investment.

Secondly, it is a triumph of incremental planning and capability-building. UPS has been implementing the IT systems that make ORION possible for the last twenty years, from online tracking and tracing to creation of detailed maps including pickup and delivery locations, to universal deployment of five generations of DIADs (Delivery Information Acquisition Device) among drivers. ORION wouldn't be possible without this infrastructure.

But perhaps most of all, the application is a change management success. UPS drivers in the US are members of the Teamsters Union, a group that is perhaps not known for its embrace of new, labor-saving technologies. But UPS spent tens if not hundreds of millions and multiple years persuading drivers, planners, supervisors, and other personnel that ORION would make their jobs better. The company even worked with the PBS science show NOVA to create a documentary on ORION, and created a variety of training programs. When you are pushing out data and analytics to the front lines, securing their understanding and buy-in of those who will use the system is critical to success.

7: REAL-TIME ANALYTICS SYSTEM TRACKS LOCOMOTIVE PERFORMANCE

#germany #europe #cargo #logistics #transportation #shipping
#freight #rail #sensor #fleet #cargo #maintenance #expense
#splunk #diagnostic #monitoring #telematics #product

D B Cargo AG is the management company for Deutsche Bahn's Rail Freight Business Unit. Deutsche Bahn bundles all national and European logistics activities by rail. DB Cargo's rail freight operation is Europe's biggest. Almost 60% of its current traffic services are pan-European and more new connections are being added. The DB cargo network now extends from Lisbon via Nizhny-Novgorod, Russia to Shenyang, China.

Transporting at least 300 million tons of cargo every year is a serious logistics challenge for DB Cargo. The company strives to drive efficiency across its operation through focus on high-quality service and reliability. The visibility into the health of its locomotives, improvement of customer experience, and reduced machine maintenance time are the priorities that need to be addressed especially at this time when the company embarks on digitization.

With its complex operations, DB Cargo has an abundance of available data coming from many sources it can use for its analysis and problem solutions. A locomotive produces 60 different time series values including temperature and engine rpm and 7,000 diagnostic data/messages from operations systems onboard telematics, component/sensor interface (including GPS), maintenance, and guidelines for locomotive operation.

To handle the large volume of diverse data in real-time, DB Cargo turned to Splunk Enterprise for a solution. The platform is now used to provide real-time insights across fleet control, operations, maintenance, and engineering. Splunk alerts are tied to a rules engine based on failure code tables. With the inputs it provides, the locomotive team can now decide the best action to take when a failure occurs. In conjunction with the locomotive manufacturers and based on the data provided, DB Cargo identifies occasions when locomotives can stay in service longer. The engineers can also recommend whether the locomotive needs to go to the maintenance workshop or not. Transparency is created in the process.

Since these measures were established, DB Cargo has been able to keep locomotives in service longer and reduce maintenance costs. These result in better delivery of service to its customers, which ultimately makes DB Cargo more competitive.

Expert Analysis by John Held,

Senior Director in Alvarez and Marsal's Digital and Technology Services practice.

What's notable is that DB Cargo has taken a real-time approach to visibility into the data and, even more importantly, tied that data to action via a business rules engine that provides direction to the locomotive team. This approach applies to industries that deal with large, expensive, and complex machinery, such as mining, constriction, shipping, and transportation. Rules engines are effective but reactive and based on expert knowledge. A more proactive approach would augment rules with machine learning that predicts future failures well before they occur. With these insights, DB could deploy maintenance teams to proactively repair and maintain equipment before field failures and breakdowns.

One area that requires special attention is that sensors and log files do not always tell the whole story. When a machine stops sending information, it could be because an operator shut it off; however, it could also result from a catastrophic electrical system failure or any other type of breakdown. The punchline is that sometimes the data you most need isn't always captured electronically, and you need simple, efficient ways for humans to provide context. Tablets and apps can enable collecting this contextual information from humans right at the point of occurrence.

Another challenge is the limits of legacy, old school technology's ability to log critical data. Retrofitting old equipment with numerous sensors can be complicated and costly. A strategy to simplify this problem is to pilot collecting many streams of information on a few locomotives, experiment on what predicts outcomes, and finally, only rollout widespread data collection based on what has proven utility.

New computing approaches like "Edge Computing" allow companies to leverage the cloud while pushing analytical storage and processing locally when it makes sense. No matter the technology, the need to assess what data is most useful to solve problems remains a priority.

DB Cargo's wealth of data will also be useful in optimizing capital investment decisions. Collecting detailed insights on locomotives' actual performance in different weather, humidity, air quality, and track conditions over time will enable DB to better procure and deploy *equipment based on its best use. DB will also develop detailed insights on supplier and manufacturer quality. If DB is better at collecting this information than anyone else, it might be potentially marketable back to manufacturers or non-competitors in the same industry and prove useful in procurement decisions and negotiations.*

8: Dialing up Big Data to Manage Annual Data Growth

#india #asia #IT #telecom #communication
#businessintelligence #analytics
#structureddata #reporting #customer

At one time, one of India's leading providers of innovative communications and mobile services, Aircel Limited, had more than 90 million subscribers nationwide. With a headquarter located in Gurgaon, Haryana, Aircel offers voice and data services, prepaid and postpaid mobile plans, broadband and wireless Internet access, and corporate communication solutions. Among its competitors, Aircel was credited with the fastest 3G roll out in the telecommunication space of India.

Just like other IT and telecom companies, Aircel counted on big data to acquire smart information and foster knowledgeable insights that can help provide sound business forecasts and more informed decision-making capabilities. In a competitive industry, accurate and timely data are essential in business growth and success.

Therefore, Aircel needed an effective solution that will help enhance database performance, improve scalability, and analyze structured data, with 10% to 15% yearly growth. The new solution will also assist in generating reports, as well as ad hoc analytical queries within existing run times.

To fulfill these requirements, Aircel chose the Vertica Analytics Platform for data loading, query execution, and backup features among others. Sanjeev Chaudhary, Business Intelligence Head of Aircel Limited, shares, "We chose Vertica as our solution of choice for the short term and the longer term as we scale. We count on this big data platform to help us innovate and solve business problems."

Vertica provided Aircel with a better performing system designed to handle multiple workloads, complex processes, and queries faster, despite its larger database size. Data off-loading has become much faster compared to previous months without Vertica tools. Additionally, as the system helped optimize data processing, support costs have become in line with Aircel's budgetary requirements for a premier data analytical solution.

As a result, Vertica not only helped ease management tasks, it also provided exceptional performance, speed, and analytical features that enabled Aircel to gather and acquire intelligent insights from structured data. This contributed to a reduction in the total cost of ownership (TCO) and annual data growth by 10 to 15%. Moreover, Vertica supports a large customer base, enabling analysis of up to 200 GBs of summarized data daily.

Expert Analysis by Peter Schooff

data evangelist, Editor-in-Chief of Data Decisioning

Aircel Limited made a terrific start implementing the Vertica Analytics Platform. The Vertica solution has delivered results in terms of speed, reducing the cost of ownership, and easing the tasks of management. These types of real results could go a long way toward promoting data democratization in the company. That means, as every Aircel employee becomes more aware of the power of data to solve business problems, intelligent insights will start being generated at all levels of the organization.

But that's only a start. To be competitive today, companies need to start harnessing the insights that come from unstructured and semi-structured data. This includes data from email, social media, video, voice, and the Internet of Things. And as all these types of data dwarf structured data in size, storage and scalability are key. But once Aircle gets a handle on these less structured types of data, it could become a telecom data powerhouse.

9: ANALYTICS HELPS MARKETING CLICK AND CONVERT

#uk #europe #TV #broadband #internet #cable #adwords
#customer #monitoring #strategy #customer

As with any other brand and business, the key to acquiring loyal customers starts with reaching out to your target audience, understanding their needs, and delivering a perfectly crafted message. TalkTalk, one of the top providers of TV, broadband, and mobile services in the UK, was in that same situation before. They wanted to grow their company and acquire more business from new and existing clients, which made them decide to gain a better understanding of their customers and use relevant campaign messages in communicating with them.

Together with its agency m/SIX, TalkTalk integrated its CRM data into Google Analytics 360 (a part of the Google Analytics 360 Suite) and other advanced analytics tools, including Google AdWords and DoubleClick Bid Manager. All these data-driven tools enabled TalkTalk to effectively gather customer insights that are useful for targeted marketing and remarketing using both display and video ads.

Analytics 360 is designed with a custom dimensions feature, which enables TalkTalk to build, monitor, and measure non-standard dimensions that are relevant to its brand. Unlike the standard free version of Google Analytics with only 20 available custom dimensions, Analytics 360 has 200 custom dimensions that TalkTalk can take advantage of. Some examples of TalkTalk's custom dimensions included customers' existing products, their eligibility to purchase other products, and the method by which the customers were recruited or invited to transact with the brand.

To measure the effectiveness of this new and analytics-based strategy, TalkTalk and m/SIX ran a remarketing campaign consisting of a test group and control group. The test group used remarketing lists from Analytics 360, while the control group only used standard URL-based remarketing.

The result of the test group showed a 63% higher click-through rate (CTR) compared to the control group based on landing page combinations and abandoned cart visits. The test group also resulted in a 219% increase in conversion rate from that of the control group, and 77% lower cost per acquisition (CPA).

Compared to traditional URL-based remarketing campaigns, the new Analytics 360 campaign produced exceptional results for TalkTalk in terms of understanding customer behavior and sending the right targeted messaging.

Expert Analysis by Kelle O'Neal,

Industry leader, data practitioner and advisor, fearless, female Founder, and CEO at First San Francisco Partners.

No doubt TalkTalk and m/SIX were pleased with such a significant increase in the conversion rate with their new approach to campaigns leveraging data and analytics. To determine just how valuable that exercise was, I'm hoping the team took it one step further to calculate the additional revenue generated by the 219% increase in conversions, compared to the control group. Wouldn't it also be nice if that test group bought more services, or higher value-added services? For less cost? Turning this into dollars and cents (or pounds and pence), would make it more real to their executives and help to justify the expense of their project and platform.

Although this story sounds simple, I'm sure there was a lot of hard work behind this first test case that should be recognized—and repurposed. Sometimes with greater flexibility and available customizations comes greater confusion and analysis paralysis. It sounds like this team focused on what data and dimensions provided relevant business value for their use case. This process, as well as the platform, could be leveraged to improve their marketing to new clients, especially new clients within a household with existing clients. This strong foundation and analytics capability may also be used to improve other sorts of customer engagement beyond marketing, into optimizing service, increasing efficiency of order management and billing, product optimization and possibly new feature development.

10: FIRE & FLAVOR GETS SWEET TASTE OF ITS ANALYTICS INVESTMENT

#usa #northamerica #food #nutrition #restaurant #AI #realtime #KPIs #monitoring #prescriptive #edi #inventory #financials

Founded in 2003 by husband and wife, Davis and Gena Knox, Fire & Flavor is a family-run food business that sells premium cooking and grilling products, including all-natural brines, cedar grilling planks, and BBQ spice rubs. Initially, they were using QuickBooks accounting solution for its robust and scalable ERP system that can run the entire business.

Several years later, they migrated to NetSuite and used its features for inventory tracking, accounting, supply planning, CRM, broker network, and payment management. They also took advantage of the Electronic Data Interchange (EDI) capability of NetSuite which enabled them to manage the orders of their trade partners.

Despite the many useful features of NetSuite, the company continued to look at other initiatives to further improve its operations. For instance, the owners wanted to gain greater visibility into its business performance across its operations and track employee KPIs in real-time, so that both management and staff could see how

28

their daily work and tasks contributed to the overall operations of the business.

To fulfill these objectives, the owners decided to utilize Okapi, an AI-driven system designed to utilize the power of data in identifying operational priorities and aligning performance with business objectives. The company took this step to pull real-time data from NetSuite, HubSpot, Google Analytics, and Mailchimp, and plot essential KPIs in a simple and comprehensible graphical presentation.

At present, instead of manually aggregating data from various tools and systems and compiling them into spreadsheets, Fire & Flavor now uses Okapi to pull in data automatically and quickly from different sources. It can now monitor KPIs in real-time, which includes revenues, operating margins, gross margins, operating, days sales outstanding, on-time shipments, email conversions, inventory accuracy, and so much more.

For Fire & Flavor, the results from shifting to Okapi's intelligent system were real and impressive. They witnessed a 94% growth in operating margins, a 92% to 98% increase in fill rate, and a 47% improvement in on-time shipping.

"We're in love with this solution. It works really well. Better yet, it lets me pat employees on the back when they do a great job," Davis Knox shared enthusiastically.

Expert Analysis by Christopher Surdak,

Chief Transformation Officer, Intelligent Automation, The Institute for Robotic Process Automation & Artificial Intelligence (IRPA AI)

Put data and insights to use: If you are not acting on your data then you are collecting cost and risk, with no benefit.

Use data at, or faster than, the speed of context change. Business Intelligence ends with a report, business analytics starts with a report.

A report is not a result, and reporting on historic performance is nothing more than digital self-flagellation.

Automate as much as possible. Intelligent Automation means getting humans out of the decision-making business and into the algorithm-writing business. Automation means stop controlling and start coordinating.

Be careful of expectations: Early wins often produce dramatic results, as the solution is new. Subsequent benefits will likely be harder-earned, but also worthwhile.

11: FLORIDA PANTHERS SCORE BIG WITH BIG DATA

#usa #northamerica #sports #athletics #competition #datamanagement #customer #datainsights #personalization #crm #marketing #campaigns

If you're managing a sports team and you want to grow its fan base, what are the things that you will do? Probably, top ideas will include TV advertisements, meet and greet concerts, charity events, and billboard advertising, right?

For Florida Panthers, they took their marketing strategy to the next level and took advantage of data-driven technology to sell more tickets, grow their fan base, and acquire sponsorship opportunities. How did they do this? They used a data management platform called Umbel to collect existing fan data from various sources, gather valuable insights, and use this information to build personalized and segmented marketing campaigns.

Initially, the Panthers gathered all their fan data from different sources, such as email lists, social media pages, ticket selling platforms, and websites. Among the data they collected from their fans using Umbel's engagement campaigns included behavior, demographics, and social brand affinities.

With these data in hand, the Panthers were able to create a more targeted approach and build custom segments. They used their fans' preferences for opposing teams or specific brands in setting up multiple segments and creating targeted messaging. After exporting these segments into their email service provider, they sent out highly targeted emails to the top 5% recipients from their database who are most likely to attend a specific game. Surprisingly, each email returned an average sales revenue of $8,711. This campaign also resulted in having the highest open and click-thru rates, and lowest cancelled subscription rate compared to previous campaigns.

The Panthers also used Umbel to run targeted ticket sales campaigns on social media. Using Umbel data, the team targeted social media users on Facebook who are closely connected to the Grateful Dead, Jerry Garcia, and other bands. This campaign resulted in a 14.6x increase in ROI.

Moreover, Umbel also played a key role in enhancing CRM records of the team which enabled them to utilize data to sell premium tickets. Even digital sponsorship on their Fan Zone website was made possible with the help of Umbel.

Overall, the Florida Panthers achieved a 12.5 increase in ROI using Umbel's data-driven platform. As the team continues to enhance their marketing strategy using data, they will further increase their opportunities to sell more tickets, acquire more fans, and drive additional sponsorship revenue.

Expert Analysis by Gokula Mishra,

Chief Data Analytics Officer at Dynamic Datalytics

This is a great use case for leveraging internal and external data to create business value—in this case Florida Panthers used data analytics to target their customers much better (rather than shooting in the dark by sending emails to everyone), and realized a bigger ROI on their campaign investment, new customer acquisition as well as increasing the basket size by sending relevant promotions.

Florida Panthers should focus on creating a flexible Identity Graph of customer data so that stitching customer data in the future will become easier as well as identifying the golden master identity will be very valuable if they do start a Loyalty program.

Also, an identity graph will enable them to use probabilistic matching to improve integrating external data thus getting better returns on the external data investments.

In order to continue to get the returns on their data analytics investment, Panthers should consider a good data governance program to manage the customer data properly (security and privacy) as well as keep the data quality fit for their business purpose.

Once they monitor the return on investment, Panthers should start assigning value to their data assets and consider sharing (for a fee) with other partners to enable more targeted sales.

12: Banking on Optimized Workload Management to Improve Response Times

#usa #northamerica #banking #investing #financial
#predictive #modeling #document #prescriptive

SunTrust Banks, Inc. is an American bank holding company. In 2019, SunTrust Banks merged with BB&T forming the holding company Truist Financial Corporation with headquarters in Charlotte, North Carolina. The merger formed the US's sixth-largest bank. SunTrust and BB&T will continue to operate under their names until their banks' systems are combined, which can take two years to complete.

The analytical modeling team within SunTrust's Client Information Group supports all lines of business. The predictive models they work on are used for important marketing activities such as for up-selling, cross-sell, and attrition are data and process-intensive.

SunTrust's old configuration encouraged significant waste of analysts' time. Because of capacity constraints, analysts usually spend time copying files from one place to another. They are also forced to wait for the completion of a batch job or a server to be available from maintenance before they can perform their regular jobs of doing analysis. The delays in reaching critical business decisions due to the inefficient use of computing resources and siloed data underscored the need for a centrally managed computing environment that effectively addresses workload management, high availability, and performance.

To address those needs, SunTrust used the SAS business intelligence and analytics platform, a grid-enabled computing architecture. SAS enables users to work in an environment where SAS applications and services are guaranteed to be available, resources are prioritized according to demand, and jobs are accelerated through parallel processing.

The grid environment now runs more efficiently where processors are better managed, and work is distributed based on available capacity and priority.

With the availability of a tool for standardized workload management and centralized administration of servers, slow response times to analytic activities are a thing of the past and important business decisions can be made as and when needed.

Expert Analysis by Nino Letteriello,

FIT Strategy & Academy Advisor. MIT CDO Symposium Committee, President of DAMA Italy and EMEA coordinator

A good story and important lesson of how successful results can be achieved when Business requirements drive Technology implementations.

In this case, all users (analysts and management alike) felt the pain of an inadequate data architecture, likely to be exacerbated by the merger; however, the challenge turned into an opportunity and

the technology solution implemented acted as enabler to a more performing data-driven organization.

The situation also offers a second and potentially more valuable opportunity. With operations now improved and those involved appreciating the benefits, it is a good time to measure the value-impact that this new decision-power has introduced into the company.

13: Reducing Time, Errors and Vision Strain in the Blink of an Eye

#usa #northamerica #banking #investing #finance
#document #machinelearning #reporting #AI #merger

JP Morgan Chase & Co. is a prestigious company that holds several significant distinctions. It is one of the oldest financial institutions in the United States.

For financial companies like JP Morgan Chase & Co., document review is a tedious process where lawyers pore over thousands of documents to determine which are relevant for litigation. It is a rote, time-consuming, and mind-numbing work for attorneys and costly for the company. The human review does not always guarantee error-free results.

The bank processes over 12,000 loan agreements per year. These documents are far less complex than contracts such as custom M&A agreements, which are better suited for human review.

JP Morgan. developed and implemented a program that runs on machine learning systems to check documents and minimize errors. They called it COIN, for Contract Intelligence. The company determined that it was good to first dispatch the program to review

37

thousands of its credit contracts. The software can review in seconds a large volume of contracts that previously took lawyers and loan officers over 360,000 person-hours. The company benefits not just from the standpoint of the cost but also quality contract review. The algorithm is more accurate than human lawyers.

JP Morgan. continues to initiate improvements to streamline the bank's system, reduce errors, and avoid redundancies. After the successful application of COIN in reviewing loan agreements, the bank appears well suited to expand its use of machine learning. It intends to deploy COIN for more complex filings.

As JP Morgan. solves its important problem for its business, it encourages a more efficient legal industry.

Expert Analysis by David Loshin,
Information Innovator Program Director at
University of Maryland iSchool

Organizations are awakening to the fact that unstructured documents contain relevant pieces of information that should be subjected to governance. From an information risk perspective, it is critical to assert some oversight that can apply an automated process to ensure compliance with defined policies. JPM's COIN solution is impressive in three key dimensions: practical value, innovation, and generalizability.

The ability to leverage automation to accurately review contracts not only reduces the need for costly human visual inspection and review, it also increases the accuracy of the review and can highlight specifics in which costly lawyers can add value. The approach is innovative in its application of advanced analytics and machine learning to a practical yet "mind-numbing" process.

I think that the most important facet of this technique is that it can be generalized to address a broader array of automated information risk management activities. JPM should be lauded for their plan to expand the use of ML and deploying COIN on more complex filings, but it could also be encouraged to use the same approach for different areas of information risk such as identifying sensitive data requiring additional protections (client privacy), self-regulation and enforcement against information exchange that poses a risk of conflicts of interest ("Chinese wall"), compliance with government regulations, or adherence to industry standards.

14: DINING ON DATA TO KEEP CUSTOMERS COMING BACK

#usa #northamerica #food #nutrition #restaurant #customer #analytics #digitaltransformation #datawarehouse #visualization #predictive #hospitality

Darden Restaurants is an American restaurant company featuring a portfolio of differentiated brands that include two specialty restaurants and six casual dining restaurants. It has more than 1,700 restaurant locations. Darden is the world's largest full-service restaurant company.

Darden's fine dining restaurants are Eddie V's Prime Seafood and The Capital Grille. Its casual dining restaurants include LongHorn Steakhouse, Olive Garden, Cheddar's Scratch Kitchen, Bahama Breeze, Season 52, and Yard House USA, Inc.

Recently, Darden has devised new ways to detect fraud, analyze customers' dinner visit duration, and optimize menu prices to save about $20 million. The company also decided it had to do more to offset and counteract declining sales particularly from its Olive Garden, Red Lobster, and LongHorn Steakhouse restaurants.

It had to boost sales and customer loyalty while pulling together data across all its restaurant operations to determine how they can perform together better.

Darden used the Check-Level Analytics tool as the first part of its digital transformation technology. The tool accumulates data on guests' experience at its restaurants such as items ordered, wait times, cook times, and pace of the meal. The data gives restaurant managers and the leaders in the corporate organization the critical information to make decisions such as optimal menus and pricing, employee development and training needs, and fraud detection.

Darden stays with its Oracle database and MicroStrategy data visualization and exploration tools. It also added new tools like Oracle Data Miner and Oracle R Enterprise, which are Oracle Advanced Analytics options to the Oracle Database. The company also decided to implement its Oracle Data Warehouse on Violin Memory, solid-state storage consisting of 10 TB of RAID on flash memory. It needs processing power and high performance as it processes over a million transactions a day from over 1,700 locations.

With its systems in place, Darden can capture vastly improved customer insights. And in doing so, it can influence guest experience and find ways to draw customers back into their restaurants. As it evolves from a rear-view to a predictive capability, it is on its way to better decision making across departments to be able to save millions.

Expert Analysis by Tom "Data Doc" Redman,
Data quality and data science advisor Data Quality Solutions

I hope that every consumer service provider in every industry reads and draws lessons from this case. The customer experience is so, so critical to your success and, for some, survival. It is easy to pay lip service to customers, even survey them from time to time. It is so much more rewarding to unpack the experience, gather and analyze some data, and find ways to make improvements. Almost everyone finds they can both improve customer satisfaction AND save money. And for some, the work is a game-changer, setting in motion a virtuous cycle that continues to uncover new opportunities.

15: ANALYTICS MAKES E-COMMERCE CLICK WITH CUSTOMERS

#india #asia #retail #entertainment #communication #customer
#social #nlp #machinelearning #prescriptive #AI

Croma is an India-based multi-branded electronic retail store run by Infiniti Retail Limited, a subsidiary of Tata Sons under Tata Enterprise, an internationally recognized brand known for providing reliable and trustworthy service. Croma's products range from home appliances, IT products, entertainment, communication, and digital imaging. In adherence to the company's tagline "We help you buy," Croma launched an eCommerce website (cromaretail.com) to promote online-offline synergies, bringing customers great benefits.

Due to the great variety of products and categories that Croma offers, it was a challenge for them to help online customers seamlessly and effectively navigate through their website and discover the most relevant products for them. Ajit Joshi, CEO & MD of Infiniti Retail Ltd., recognized this problem and reiterated that because of the broad range of their product selections, customers were having a hard time looking for what they needed, and as a result, conversions suffered.

The company explored traditional ways to address the problem. They considered using recommendation methods that rely on the history of customer clicks on the website and their purchase history. Although these methods may have worked on older products, it was not applicable to newly posted products since there were no initial data about these products. A possible remedy to the flaw of these methods was to manually promote new products but doing so was an unnecessary hassle.

Finally, Croma decided to partner with Infinite Analytics that utilizes a multi-dimensional approach to personalize recommendations to individual customers. It uses a mix of semantic technologies, NLP, and machine learning methods to understand Croma's products better. Insights regarding the customers' evolving preferences, tastes, and affinities are analyzed using their brand affinity, social profile, recent activities, macroeconomic and household data. These two analyses are then combined to help the online retailer to comprehend the intent of the user.

After only six months Croma started reaping significant improvements in its e-commerce website. Their revenue share increased by 25%, orders with recommendations increased by nearly 30%, and their conversions increased by 217%.

Expert Analysis by Farouk Ferchichi,

Chief Data & Analytics Officer at Envestnet, Inc

The impact on the revenue share and its parts attribution to the recommendations stands out to me as many data analytics production have a hard time measuring the incremental value to the organization. The cultural shift that the organization made, swift, in understanding that their business/digital transformation won't be possible without an effective use of analytics. Furthermore, their ability to test and learn quickly and shifting both the approach to data analytics leverage e.g., historical to ML-based as well as engaging a third party, who seemed qualified and trusted partner.

I am certain that the operational decision of leveraging analytics to drive business outcome e.g., revenue wasn't easy, aligning with CFO to attribute value isn't easy, and partnering with a third-party to own such a critical functionality that has such impact to the organization. In summary, internal operational alignment, financial alignment, and third-party alignment—required a heavy change management work.

Going forward, I would recommend a couple things: 1) On tech front: more data sources, coupled with a focus on product/channel/customer matching optimization model 2) Explore a multi-channel delivery of the analytics not just thru web but mobile, IVR, contact centers, etc. coupled with a solid conversational AI capabilities investment and a continuous ability to measure incremental value. Also, I can't help but wonder about the question of accountabilities of business outcomes and incentive model as we move forward and learn that businesses of all kind data analytics is going to be a critical production into how products are designed and sold.

16: WORKSPACE SOLUTION SALES ANALYTICS JUST WORKS

#usa #northamerica #software #tech #mdm #dataquality
#customer #predictive #diagnostic #crm #dataintegration

Citrix *is an American multinational* software company specializing in desktop, application, server virtualization, networking, cloud computing, and software as a service (SaaS) technology.

Like most companies, Citrix looked to growth the number of customers who would take advantage of its workspace solutions. So the focused on boosting the effectiveness of their marketing campaigns, improving lead-to-opportunity conversion rates, and launching targeted offers to the right people at the right time. Citrix also wanted to gain a view of its existing customer relationships to be able to analyze them and further improve their working relationships.

Though the strategy was in place, the biggest challenge that the company faced was the quality and accuracy of its data. For instance, data on prospects, customers, and channel partners, including account and contact information, were either inaccurate, incomplete, or duplicated in the CRM system. This led to slow data acquisition, inaccurate information, error-prone efforts, and wasted marketing strategies due to lacking or incomplete prospect data.

To overcome this roadblock, Citrix needed to pull together existing data from the various sources and systems they were using. These include Salesforce, Marketo, and an in-house customer portal. The company then transitioned to using Informatica MDM to generate clean, accurate, and integrated data on channel partners, customers, and prospects, including the relationships among them which will be helpful in operational applications.

By leveraging analytics from this integrated data, Citrix recognized 20% growth and efficiency in lead-to-opportunity conversion rates. The company also achieved a 50% increase in the quality of data it receives at the point of entry, as well as a 50% reduction in the acquisition rate of duplicate and junk data for prospects, contacts, and existing accounts. Moreover, Citrix was able to deliver a better experience to both their customers and channel partners by renewing all user licenses across product lines and identifying new opportunities for upselling.

Expert Analysis by John K. Thompson,

Best-selling author, data and analytics thought leader, innovator, and practitioner, and global head of advanced analytics and artificial intelligence, CSL Behring

Citirix has encountered, and overcome, one of the most common stumbling blocks to the effective, efficient, and continuous use of data in enterprises around the world, lack of data integration and lack of data quality and integrity. One of the most challenging problems that enterprises face before they can begin to address data quality and data integration is the approach and mindset that pervades the leadership of the organization. Leader often think, and believe, that if they commission and undertake a one-time project that the data quality and integration problem will be resolved; this is not the case.

All organizations that intend to use their various data assets on a regular basis for marketing, sales, supply chain, manufacturing improvement and more need to have an on-going program that is funded and staffed with one of the primary objectives of the program to produce and deliver cleaned, integrated and well-managed enterprise data that is treated as a valued asset. Once you have a robust master data management function and team, then waves of accurate, useful and actionable analytics can be built to drive the organization forward across all functional and operational units of the organization.

From this case study, it appears to me that Citrix realized their need for integrated, cleaned and well-maintained data. The world has moved past the era where focusing on one primary source of data will suffice. Citrix is bringing together and integrating multiple sources of data. This is a foundational need for programs like customer outreach, warranty management, sales, marketing, product management and more. Beyond these more transactional purposes, enterprise organizations need to have an on-going program of ingesting, cleaning and integrating internal and external data sources for analytical purposes. When data is available for transactional and analytical purposes, innovation and exploration can flourish and drive competitive advantage each and every day, and isn't that why we have data and analytics, to provide an edge over our competitors?

17: German Football Team Kicks Off Advanced Analytics Project

#germany #europe #sports #athletics #competition
#football #soccer #reporting #video #performance

The German National Football Team is one of the world's most successful football teams in international competitions. It has earned 4 FIFA World Cup titles—in 1954, 1974, 1990, and 2014. Aside from gold, the team has also won 4 silver and 3 bronze medals in the FIFA World Championships. A team in the UEFA Europe Confederation, the team has also emerged victorious in three European Championships, having won the championships in 1972, 1980, and 1996. The German team has also won the Confederations Cup once, in 2017.

At the end of the 2014 World Cup, Germany earned a record of 2,205 points in the Elo rating, the highest of any national football team in history. In 2013, the German Football Association (DFB) and SAP announced a partnership to improve the business processes of the national football federation.

The German national football team wanted to capitalize on the opportunity to use big data in an early adoption phase for preparation for the World Cup 2014 in Brazil. It wanted to mine post analyses data from matches to improve the team's and players' performance for the upcoming World Cup.

The technology is provided by SAP through "SAP Match Insights," a HANA-based platform that is designed to facilitate the analysis, training, and preparing for tournaments. It also greatly aids coaches to make use of vast amounts of data to assess key situations in each match to improve the player and team performances. A 10-minute match scenario involving 10 players with three balls can produce over 7 million data points. SAP HANA can process this data in real-time. With SAP, the team can analyze huge amounts of data to customize its training and prepare better for the next match. Additional insights are aimed to benefit the media, enabling them to deliver a better-informed, more interesting commentary.

The German national football team used the technology before its world cup game against a strong Portugal team. In that Group G game, Germany beat Portugal 4–0. Also, it was learned that before the match against Portugal, German player Jerome Boateng received several key scenes with Cristiano Ronaldo on his app so he could study and prepare for Ronaldo's every move in the penalty area.

Moreover, using data and analytics, the German team determined how to reduce individual possession time from 3.4 seconds to 1.1. seconds, a critical improvement that is credited with helping the team defeat Brazil in the semi-finals and Argentina for the championship.

Recently, the SAP-German National Team partnership has been extended to collaborate on developing a software-based solution to enhance the on-field performance of the national football team.

Expert Analysis by Milan Kucera,

Contractor: CSV, QA/Compliance (FDA, EU), Pharmacy Regulatory. 25+ years of experience in Information technology with major emphasis on information quality management, process improvement

ELO rating/coefficient is a statistical approach evaluating player or team performance. Method was developed by Arpad Elo and applied on chess players at the first time. Using this method of measuring performance of the football (soccer) teams was a great idea, how to compare teams around the World to establish a World list. It is as well applied on players from the German Bundesliga by Arndt & Brefeld in 2016.

It is possible to imagine how much data must be collected and what an effort is necessary to ensure that all used data are complete (for men's and women's teams), and more significantly—accurate, verified. These are minimum requirements on data entered to the system to provide necessary calculations. The system is backed by sophisticated statistical mathematics. In fact, fans and others can validate all calculations which were presented in an online table (e.g. FIFA Cocal Cola World ranking: https://www.fifa.com/fifa-world-ranking/ranking-table/men/).

Open question concerning this model is how to standardize it across all national federations. If they are already using their own model versus the FIFA model, what differences are there, what will happen when the model is modified or changed. Must all results be recalculated? And what would be the economic impact of the team if a calculation is using inaccurate or incomplete data?

Football (soccer) is a business like any other in which investors, owners, and others have their own economic interests. Data and analytics are critical for team configuration, procedures and performance improvement.

18: Decoding Customer Dark Data for Targeted Offers

#turkey #asia #europe #banking #commercial #retail #corporate #financial #crm #reporting #customer #product #prediction #marketing

AK Bank is one of the largest banks in Turkey. The bank's subsidiaries provide non-banking financial services, capital markets, and investment services. AK Bank has been consistently ranked as "The Most Valuable Banking Brand in Turkey" by "Brand Finance—Banking 500."

AK Bank has been an innovator in online and app-driven products and unique branch strategies. It has been recognized globally for its innovations. As any bank, AK Bank works to anticipate changes in customer dynamics and trends, and to develop products that serve customers' unique and changing needs.

Its customer relationship management (CRM) solution was successful in capturing customer information to target market them. However, this brought with it a dilemma for the bank. Its customer offers increased 15-fold in the last six years with 300,000 inbound product sales per month. Too many marketing messages were confusing and even aggravating customers.

The bank sought analytic methods that would determine what to offer to the right customers through the right channels at the right time. And this solution needed to build upon the existing CRM solution investment and groundwork. The campaign solution needed to use all its customer data in an integrated structure, evaluate different suited campaigns, and devise different scenarios based on a wide variety of parameters. Clear and concise reporting was also required for this solution.

Using previous years' data, AK Bank was able to predict the impact of constraints. It took advantage of SAS RDBMS to perform detailed modeling and 'what if' analysis using a high-performance optimization engine. Today, the bank produces better-targeted communications that have slashed its campaign costs by 50%. And it can now evaluate a high number of possible campaigns in a fraction of the time. Optimization processes that once took 2.5 days now take 2.5 hours, and have led to significant revenue increases.

Expert Analysis by Mario Faria,

VP, Research Board for Chief Data and Analytics Officers at Gartner

One of the main problems for financial services organizations, especially for those who have been on business for a long time is to modernize their current infrastructure to support the new demands from customers. Customers today are not as loyal as they used to be in the past. With a few clicks of a mouse, a customer can open a service with a competitor, and transfer the funds to start a new work relationship.

More than ever, it becomes mandatory for banks to have a successful omnichannel strategy, where one can map the customer journey, and see what is working and what can be improved.

And the best model to create this omnichannel strategy is to surround the legacy infrastructure with modern tools and to implement new processes. There is a better ROI in doing that, and a shorter time to bring to market the new solutions:

I can see a few positive actions AK Bank did. They were able to map their customers to the right offerings and direct the customers to the right channels. They were able to use the CRM and SAS to model and to simulate scenarios that will help them to plan for actions in each one of them. They reduce the cost of serving customers, and probably, besides increasing profitability, the customer satisfaction increased through time.

19: Exploiting Data and Analytics to Fight Child Exploitation

#usa #northamerica #global #sextrafficking #dataintegration
#machinelearning #AI #webharvesting #text #document #monitoring

Previously known as the DNA Foundation when it was founded in 2009, Thorn is an international anti-human trafficking organization whose mission is to address the sexual exploitation of children. It describes its organization as "Digital Defenders of Children." It was founded to devise smart, digital strategies for protecting children from harmful and illegal activities, such as sex trafficking, pornography, and sex tourism.

This NGO, founded by actors Demi Moore and Ashton Kutcher, focuses on internet technology and its role in the proliferation of child pornography and sexual slavery of children on a global scale.

Based on Thorn's research, child sex trafficking victims now are advertised and sold primarily via the internet—but with falsified identities and ages. The amount of data is enormous, and its highly inconsistent nature makes the detection of illegal activity very difficult for law enforcement. The challenge for the organization was to analyze ads collected from online commercial sex marketplaces to identify likely cases of child sexual exploitation, the victims, and exploiters.

Thorn called on two of its technology partners, Connotate (now Import.io) and Digital Reasoning for support. Import.io's solution harvests and transforms web data and content into high-value information assets, enabling mass data aggregation, migration, and integration. And Digital Reasoning offers a machine-learning platform that automates the understanding of human communications. The collaboration between Thorn and its partners presented the possibility of a breakthrough solution.

Connotate and Digital Reasoning team created an application called Spotlight that enables Thorn to collect content from classified ad sites and then analyze illegal ad offerings. The tool uses a combination of web-harvesting and advanced text analytics to identify suspicious ads.

The team demonstrated that public online data, when scrutinized using smart analytics technology, does include subtle clues that can help identify minors.

With algorithms analyzing thousands of pages of content, law enforcement officers can focus their precious attention on the most likely violations. The technology learns from real-world investigations and gets smarter to facilitate more informed decision-making the more often it is used.

The Spotlight tool has been used in over 800 investigations and has resulted in the identification of 300 victims and more than 50 sex traffickers. The tool is currently used by more than 1800 law enforcement officers across the United States.

Expert Analysis by Phil Simon,

Keynote speaker, collaboration and technology authority, college professor, and author of eleven books, including Analytics: The Agile Way and Reimagining Collaboration: Slack, Microsoft Teams, Zoom, and the Post-COVID World of Work

Data deity Jeffrey Hammerbacher famously quipped, "The best minds of my generation are thinking about how to make people click ads. That sucks."

He wasn't wrong, but this story illustrates a decidedly non-commercial application of contemporary analytics and related methods. I'm all for making a buck, but we can—nay, need—to address public-health crises with a more analytical bent than we have in years past. Ditto for new data-visualization tools and data sources—particularly unstructured data. Relying exclusively upon old-school data sources, methods, applications, and intuition will only get us so far.

20: Major Shipping Company Transports its Business with a Wave of Data-Driven Efficiencies

#denmark #europe #global #worldwide #logistics #shipping #freight #transportation #supplychain #intelligentdata #dataanalytics #analytics #advancedanalytics #predictive #monitoring #sensors

A.P. Moller—Maersk is an integrated container logistics company. A worldwide conglomerate that operates in 130 countries, is is involved in a wide range of industries including shipping, logistics, and oil and gas. It has its headquarters in Copenhagen, Denmark, it owns Maersk Line, the world's largest shipping company with 600 vessels transporting hundreds of billions of dollars' worth of goods per year.

Maersk has been operating for over 100 years, building on its deep knowledge and experience within shipping and logistics, crossing both continents and supply chains. Still, Maersk constantly explores new ways to innovate and grow with its customers. It also continues to create new connections between people, processes, and intelligent data; making every supply chain both simpler and better connected.

The biggest challenge for Maersk has always been to sustain profitability. The shipping industry has not been the same since the 2008 financial crisis, nor the recent pandemic. These macroeconomic events resulted in decreased trade, increased tendency of multinational companies to build local factories, and tighter competition. Moreover, the industry has been plagued with overcapacity, putting pressure on freight prices.

It is especially critical for shipping companies to differentiate themselves through data and analytics. Maersk has done exactly this by building the Maersk Advanced Analytics Team that focuses on big data projects. The Team continues to work on areas critical to Maersk's long-term profitability and survival. Among the areas it has applied big data analytics to bring about improvements include:

- *Fuel efficiency: Fuel consumption is one of the largest costs for Maersk.*

- *Customer targeting: The right customer targeting maximizes the value of goods shipped.*

- *Load efficiency: The Analytics group discovered that the company spends about $1 billion a year just to move empty containers.*

- *Predictive maintenance: Downtimes from engine breakdowns are among the biggest revenue killers.*

Close monitoring of vessels' voyage speed and enhanced analytics resulted in Maersk achieving a reduction in fuel consumption of 13% in just two years. Advanced analytics has been increasing commercial sales through better customer targeting. The number of boxes the company carried has increased by 11% over that same period.

The $1 billion a year the company spends to move empty containers is practically eliminated using optimized planning using analytics tools. Additionally, Maersk installed sensors that alert when engines need service, rather than waiting for breakdowns. Not only have longer downtimes been prevented, but engine efficiency has been improved overall. In total, these data-driven improvements have had a financial impact in hundreds of millions of dollars.

Expert Analysis by Herman Heyns,

CEO at Anmut

It is a real value driven case study and I suspect the data and analytics team know there is still further to go. My sense is there is another $2-$3 billion of additional value per year that can be realised through data and analytics, and a total overall data value in excess of $20 billion. The question is how to realise that, now the low-hanging fruit has been picked? This kind of question demands a value-focused approach. One that starts with proper data valuation, which reveals the priority data assets, what needs to happen to release additional value, and signals to the business the scale of the value at stake. From there, it's a case of establishing good management discipline around the assets and focusing on growing the value from there.

My recommendations going forward would be to:

- *Do a proper data valuation to identify the most critical data assets.*

- *Demonstrate the potential of further value from these data assets.*

- *Ensure there is Exec level ownership of each high value data asset.*

- *Measure the condition and required state to release the additional value.*

- *Prioritise the investment into the highest value assets, compare data on a like for like basis with ships and other investments.*

- *Track progress as if if each data asset were a business unit.*

21: Substituting Data for Inventory

#germany #europe #ecommerce #mcommerce #retail

#finance #banking #realestate #machinelearning

#consumer #customerservice #deeplearning

#predictive #reporting #AI #automation

The Otto Group or Otto Gmbh & Co KG is a €13 billion private mail-order, retail e-commerce company and currently one of the world's biggest e-commerce companies, operating in more than 20 countries worldwide.

As a shareholder, Otto Group engages in a variety of e-commerce services. it owns 3 Suisses, claimed to be the leading e-commerce business in France, and has expanded into financial services and real estate.

Otto started using big data and machine learning for customer management. Already it had been efficiently collecting data and analyzing the information to understand consumer tastes, recommend products, and personalize its website for customers. However, the most pressing opportunity was to minimize the returns of products, which cost the company millions of euros per year.

Otto's conventional data analysis identified two major causes of customer returns and order cancellation: 1) Customers receiving their merchandise beyond two days of ordering, and 2) Customers not receiving all its orders at once but in multiple shipments.

Since Otto sells merchandise from other brands, it does not stock those items itself. Hence, it finds it difficult to avoid shipping delays until the complete orders are ready for fulfillment and lots of boxes delivered at different times.

The typical solution entails improved forecasting by buyers as to what customers are going to buy then advanced ordering such goods. Otto did better, however, by creating a system employing Blue Yonder's deep-learning algorithm originally developed for a particle-physics experiment at the Geneva CERN Laboratory. The system analyzes 3 billion past transactions and 200 variables, including past sales, searches on Otto website, weather info, etc. to predict what customers will buy a week in advance of its ordering.

The AI system has proven to be highly reliable. It can predict with 90% accuracy the merchandise that will be sold within 30 days. Otto now permits the purchase of around 200,000 items from third-party brands automatically, without human intervention. This has resulted in a 20% decline in Otto's surplus stock that it holds in its inventory.

Expert Analysis by Peggy K. Tsai,

Chief Data Officer at BigID, Top 50 Women in Tech Influencer, co-author of *The AI Book*, and data governance practitioner

Otto Group can continue to improve its machine learning accuracy rate of 90% through collection of more data on the customer returns and by continuing to analyze the customer preferences and buying

patterns. They can also analyze customer sentiment from social media channels and on website/feedback forms to improve insights.

Additionally, Otto can proactively aim to target its customers and build better customer recommendation engines by using the same AI system for customer returns. By applying the same machine learning techniques at the beginning of the customer experience journey, Otto can reduce errors and costs later on.

Otto's usage of machine learning in the online retail experience is on-par with other retailers who are leveraging machine learning technologies to understand large scale data on a real-time basis. They may consider leveraging cloud computing to gain efficiencies and depending on the sourcing of the data, edge computing for improved computing times and analytics.

22: Know-Your-Customer Solution Provides a Royal Boost to Customer Service

#UK #europe #banking #insurance #finance
#financialservices #customer #chatbots #personalization

The Royal Bank of Scotland Group (RBS), is a £14.143 billion British banking and insurance holding company. It provides a wide range of services such as personal and business banking, corporate finance, and insurance to personal, commercial and large corporate and institutional accounts through its offices located in Europe, North America and Asia, employing 67,000 individuals worldwide. It operates a wide variety of banking brands. Headquartered in Edinburg, Scotland, its main subsidiaries in the UK are The Royal Bank of Scotland, NatWest, NatWest Markets, Ulster Bank, and Coutts.

RBS handles an enormous amount of information from its transactions and interactions with customers, including account changes, calls, and webchat. It realized the need to analyze customer activities holistically to personalize service for different types of customers. The information from each of these varying customer touchpoints offered important insight into how RBS can optimize the customer experience.

Recently, online chat has become the preferred customer communication channel of RBS's customers. Therefore, it wanted to use this unstructured communications log to build a holistic picture of customer activity and communication.

With the aid of Trifacta, RBS utilized data wrangling to transition raw data source inputs into prepared outputs to be utilized in the analysis. The process was optimized and the data structurally analyzed, enabling the agents to be intelligently-informed on how to best interact with customers online.

Analysts can now intuitively leverage diverse customer data to build a 360-degree view of their clients. Moreover, the time spent by the agents on data preparation for customer interaction has been reduced by 15x.

Expert Analysis by Daragh O Brien
CEO/Managing Director at Castlebridge

This vignette highlights the importance of understanding the information value chain. Customer interactions in chat were not disposable scripted events but were recognised as a source of information and intelligence about the customer and their needs. This is the same impetus that drove historic CRM strategies from the late 1990s to build systems to capture interactions with the customer. As such, care needs to be taken to avoid the types of mistakes we were making twenty years ago taming call centre and email interactions. That means needing to have a clear understanding of who and what a customer is and being able to map free-text interactions to categories of need or issue so that customer service agents get actionable information.

For an organisation as diverse as RBS that has grown through acquisition one key challenge will be rolling this technology out across all their disparate divisions in a consistent manner. What works well in one locale may not work well in another. Linguistic and other factors in text analysis will need to be considered. The ability to provide agents with a better understanding of the customer's issues and needs in a timelier manner doesn't just reduce time spent on preparation. It translates directly into a bottom-line impact in terms of cost of customer service.

Organisations struggle to get staff internally to input data in a consistent manner. Free text chat with customer input is an order of magnitude higher. So data quality and the ability to train the analytics processes to wrangle the data were likely key areas of challenge to be overcome. Part of that challenge would be linguistic quirks and dialect issues in the input data. To an American, "Yeah, right!" might look like an affirmation of positivity. To an Irish person, we see a potentially strong negative sentiment.

Other challenges would include implementing the chat technology in a way that balances organisational efficiency with requirements of data protection law and other regulatory requirements in financial services. Another key challenge that this type of technology can raise is the ethical issue of digital exclusion, either through literacy issues (people not being able to understand the text-driven interactions) or through technology access issues (people not being able to bank online due to connectivity or other issues). For an essential service like banking, this needs to be borne in mind as service delivery is optimised so that the macro-infonomic impact of better data use doesn't create unwanted results.

The mining of 'conversational' data such as this could be used to not only prepare the agent but also to prepare the customer. The same data could be used to identify interaction types that could be streamed to a self-service channel, or smart chatbots could be used to enable customers to self-serve in the chat environment, saving human agents for the high-complexity/high-touch transaction types that really need to have human input. Of course, the challenge is doing this in a way that doesn't alienate customers by over-optimising the experience to the benefit of the bank but to the detriment of the customer.

23: Real-Time Data and Predictive Tool Help Reduce Violent Attacks by 50%

#usa #northamerica #correctionalfacilities #prison #datamanagement
#realtime #visualization #monitoring #reporting #dashboard

Violent attacks could happen to just about anyone, even to the people designated to stop those kinds of attacks. An environment where criminals are supposed to reflect on their crimes is also when brutal assaults against several staff members commonly happen. For 18 months, at least 320 violent assaults were reported monthly across the Indiana Department of Correction's (IDOC) adult facilities.

The number of cases involving violent attacks on correctional officers and staff members was disturbing. Not only was it a danger to the life of the people working within the facility, but it was also a burden in terms of compensation and productivity.

It became apparent that the current risk assessment tool was not working well anymore. The Indiana Risk Assessment System (IRAS) merely uses static information captured at the input to predict violence. The system failed to combine ongoing and critical changes to prisoners' risk status. A low-risk prisoner could always turn into a high-risk prisoner, and vice-versa. The facility needed a new tool that's designed to find and communicate when offenders are most volatile and would systematically lessen violent assaults on guards and even fellow inmates.

IDOC)decided to deploy data management tools from SAS to integrate and aggregate data from different systems, including IRAS)and its offender information management system, including several near-real-time risk factors. And according to researcher Sarah Schelle, the system now overlooks the bias of demographics and focuses on how they can change with the help of rehabilitation and policy.

Each adult correctional facility now has access to the analytics containing the material risk data. This enables custody, mental health, and even program staff members to discuss specific prisoners weekly to determine the best course of action. By identifying which factors caused the particular prisoner to become a high-risk one, the IDOC)can quickly address issues to mitigate and reduce these types of incidents from occurring again.

The new risk assessment tool is working as planned. Compared to IRAS), the new tool is four times more accurate in predicting violence. As a result, staff assaults dropped by 50% during the first six months. And inmate-on-inmate assaults dropped by 20%.

Another benefit the new system presented to the IDOC was time savings. Before, the IRAS)model would take the staff at least 13,000 hours per week to scan and process all 27,000 inmates efficiently.

Expert Analysis by George Firican,

Founder LightsOnData, Director Data Governance and Business Intelligence at UBC

There are three great takeaways from this case study. The first take-away is that having near-real-time data and different integrated systems to enrich the existing data set, can create a more robust analytical model. The second take-away is that the data and information accessibility provided to cross functional teams allowed a more comprehensive view of the issues and their potential solutions. Lastly, we often see the impact that data, data management, and analytics have on a business's bottom line, but we forget about the impact these have on people's lives and wellbeing. This story offers a great example of the importance of data and how treating it as an asset can sometimes be life changing for their stakeholders.

Going forward, IDOC should keep in mind that these data management and analytics efforts are not a one-time initiative, but a continuous endeavour. As such, they should consider regular audits of their data, processes, and analytical model. For continuous improvement, outliers should be analyzed closely and fed back into the model, as opposed to disregarded, and start collaborating with other correctional facilities to share data and findings.

24: REAL TIME FRAUD ANALYTICS IS IN THE CARDS

#usa #northamerica #financialservices #banking
#transaction #investment #credit #merchant
#hadoop #machinelearning #dataanalytics #modeling
#dataintegration #customerloyalty #monitoring

American Express (Amex) is an American multinational financial services corporation that is best known for its credit card, charge card, and traveler's cheque businesses. It is the leading financial services company, privy to $1 trillion of point of sales data every year and roughly 5–7 billion transactions. The American Express network accounts for almost a quarter of the total dollar volume transacted in the United States, and processes transactions from over 100 million active credit cards worldwide.

American Express follows a closed-loop system wherein its banking subsidiaries act as both the issuer and acquirer, giving the company the benefit of viewing all transactions on the customer and merchant side, real-time.

Amex decided to modernize its data and analytics capabilities as a foundation for achieving an advantage in its delivery of innovative products and provide value to customers. Its Risk & Information Management team and the company's Technology group collaborated to build world-class Big Data capabilities. They moved from traditional database technology to a Hadoop infrastructure and implemented machine learning algorithms to optimize decision making— particularly for detecting fraud and bringing customers and merchants closer together.

Using various customer and related data streams and sources, evolving pattern-matching algorithms now can flag transactions with a high risk of being fraudulent in real-time, rather than retroactively.

Its system can analyze trends and information on cardholder spending and build algorithms to provide customized offers to attract and retain customers. Amex also leverages information to maintain the relationship with merchants. Through its targeted marketing program Amex Offers, it can match merchants with the right customers. What used to be a three-day process is now reduced to 20 minutes.

To-date, Amex has identified and squashed over $2 billion in potential annual incremental fraud incidents. Within two years of its launch, the Amex Offers program saved cardholders a combined $100 million.

Expert Analysis by James Kobielus

Senior Research Director, Data Management at TDWI

Amex is addressing both top-line revenue enhancement (customize offers to attract and retain customers) and bottom-line cost avoidance (identified billions in potential annual incremental fraud incidents) with a single initiative.

Amex is doing all this in a real-time closed-loop system that drives both target marketing and fraud detection through application of machine learning to customer data.

This is exemplary of what many similar financial services companies have done and are doing today. What would have been interesting is if they had disclosed how they are "evolving algorithms in real-time" (e.g., done real-world experiments inline to these business processes to test different machine learning models and deploy the best-fit models operationally). If would also have been interesting if they'd discussed the differences between the specific machine learning models used for the specific use cases (fraud prevention, churn mitigation, target marketing, customer experience optimization) implicit in this case study, since it's almost certain they're not using the same specific ML models for each of these.

The principal challenge—chewing up time, money, and technical personnel—would have been consolidating, cleansing, and preparing all of their customer data in the Hadoop data lake. What's not stated in this case is whether, considering the cost of doing all that and instituting ongoing data governance, the entire initiative is net positive on Amex's bottom line, or, if it has been, how long they took to break even on it.

The next level in any such financial services initiative is to bring this front-office/back-office closed-loop process into a self-service business model. This would ensure that Amex customers, from their mobile apps and in their browsers, have a secure unified experience in which to receive targeted offers, manage their accounts, and track how well Amex is protecting them by sniffing for and pre-empting fraud.

25: Speaking of Real Time
Decision Making...

#spain #southamerica #global #telecommunications
#smartphone #broadband #cable #television
#predictive #machinelearning #marketing #AI

Telefonica is a Spanish telecommunications company that provides mobile, fixed, broadband and telecommunications services to 347 million customers in 21 countries it operates in or has a presence within. It is Europe's largest telecommunications company and the fifth largest in the world.

Headquartered in Madrid, Telefonica employs 125,000 professionals and has 349 million accesses worldwide. It includes the brands Telefonica, Movistar, O2 and Vivo. Telefonica Chile, called Movistar, offers fixed telephone, mobile and long-distance services; Internet access and switching via broadband ADSL and VDSL; DTH satellite television; transport services satellite radio and TV, and Fiber optics and IPTV services.

Telefonica's transformation to become an 'Online Telco', an efficient company that gives its clients the possibility of being connected with what they want most and love, among other major objectives, started.

In line with this transformation objective, Telefonica Chile realized that it needed to address the challenges they face from the market. Stronger competition was emerging, resulting to increase in churn or customer attrition, higher operational costs, and other unwanted developments.

At that time, Telefonica Chile was doing the traditional practice of sending automated outbound campaigns periodically. It was inefficient as they didn't really meet the needs of the customers at the particular moment. Even utilizing predictive machine learning to aid in improving the rates of outbound campaigns was not good enough to be proactive.

Telefonica Chile moved to a real-time system for contextual marketing. It used two software in series: SAS Event Stream Processing (ESP), which reads massive data from CDR and antennas; and SAS Real-Time Decision Manager (RTDM), which receives "golden resulting events" that trigger certain responses.

After being applied for the first time using just seven cases, the system generated an additional $2 million average revenue in the first four months. The return on the investments for the system was achieved in a short time, as a result. Telefonica Chile has since been implementing this system for addressing a real marketing problem as it realizes value from Big Data.

The company's roadmap considers applying real-time machine learning algorithms to improve response rates through the generation of adaptive messages to customers.

Expert Analysis by Peter Dehaan,

Lecturer, consultant and owner, Innov8 Biz

If this pandemic has taught us nothing else, saving money should not be the only outcome we seek to achieve. Building healthier and more comfortable buildings can improve occupant safety, productivity and satisfaction which can make a building a more desirable environment for occupants to inhabit.

This case study highlighted the importance of trusted data and how to best use it. However, if the project had expanded its horizons before refining the scope other possibilities could have been identified that may have been cost effective during the HVAC upgrade. Many HVAC systems are often designed before occupancy and usage is known, and many buildings suffer from hot and cold zones, while other systems try to reduce running cost at the expense of fresh air turnover, while occupants of some buildings seem to have more sick days.

This additional data could have been quickly collected by listening to the building occupants, and some of this data could have been quantified by the deployment of IoT devices which are getting cheaper every year. The real trick here, however, is around having the vision and the data literacy skills to maximise the value of the data being collected. Pieces of data individually only provide a small piece of the puzzle, having the skills to bring together and interpret the bigger picture is one of the keys to being more effective in the 21st Century.

Through the use of IoT devices and data literacy, how many buildings could be made more habitual for occupants, and cheaper to run?

26: A FLOOD OF DATA PREVENTS WATER-RELATED ENVIRONMENTAL INCIDENTS

#UK #europe #utilities #infrastructure #water #predictive #recommendation #modeling #sustainability #operationaldata

Thames Water Utilities Ltd. (TWUL) is the largest water and wastewater service company in the UK. It is a Reading, Berkshire-based monopoly private utility company that provides water supply and wastewater treatment services for 15 million people daily. It serves large parts of Greater London including Thames Valley, Luton, Gloucestershire, Surrey, Kent, and other areas of the United Kingdom.

TWUL believes that environmental protection, including the responsible and sustainable use of natural resources, is fundamental to its business. One of its strategies is to develop the use of operational data to better manage its network, including applying new techniques to predict leaks and floods to enable them to be more proactive in their response.

In keeping with its proactive position in response to environmental threats, Thames Water Utilities Ltd. uses predictive analytics to gain an understanding of how flooding and pollution incidents occur in the utility holes in its wastewater network. The learning from this investigation is aimed to avoid costly leakages, bad company publicity, dissatisfied customers, and most importantly, create a cleaner environment.

Thames Water Utility used the IBM SPSS Modeler as a tool to establish a predictive model to analyze incident data and determine the utility holes most prone to flooding and cause pollution problems. Holes with a history of flooding or located near watercourses were looked at especially. Through the analysis, the company was able to identify access points that needed to undergo preventive maintenance that included activities from cleaning pipes to replacing faulty water mainlines.

Predictive modeling increased the precision of identifying maintenance holes that are most at risk of flooding and causing a pollution incident. These utility holes were prioritized for preemptive maintenance. Thames Water Utility Ltd expects that over a two-year period, it will be able to prevent 120 pollution incidents from the maintenance of 2,000 utility holes. The financial benefits to be realized from a reduction in regulatory fines are estimated to be about US$4.7 million annually, a 33% reduction.

Expert Analysis by James Price
Founder and Managing Director at Experience Matters

Few organisations have the ability or willingness to determine the cost of managing their Information Assets (their data, information, content and knowledge), the value of those assets or the benefit that managing those assets well delivers. There are many reasons for this as identified in research conducted and published by Experience Matters and the University of South Australia.

But the most important of those reasons is a lack of business governance around those assets. At every monthly Board meeting, directors demand to see the financial reports of how well the financial assets are being managed. But they never, ever ask to see the information reports of how well the information assets are being managed. Thames Water Utilities has identified benefits from leveraging its information assets that are sufficiently substantial to attract managerial attention—and that is commendable.

Thames Water Utilities was likely to have faced challenges in the areas of asset governance and responsibility, leadership and management, business governance and accountability, executive awareness, benefits realisation, justification, leverage and exploitation of the data, data quality, and corporate behaviours.

I would like to see the development of models that enable organisations to justify the investment in the continuous improvement of the quality of their information assets.

27: A Shaky Way to Optimize Equipment Utilization

#netherlands #europe #mentalhealth #healthcare #health
#sensors #analytics #monitoring #recommendation #employee

G GZ Nederland (Dutch Association for Addiction and Mental Health) is an association that represents about a hundred affiliate member organizations in the mental health care industry in the Netherlands.

The association, consisting of various large regional and small specialized care providers, continues to grow and gain more members through the years. The combined turnover of its member organizations is over €5 billion. A total of 89,000 work in mental health care in the Netherlands and GGZ has more than 90% of care and mental health care personnel among its members.

GGZ Nederland strives to make good national agreements with the stakeholders—government, politicians, insurers, patient organizations, and other partners so that member institutions are given the space to deliver efficient and innovative mental healthcare and to maintain high quality.

Dutch Association for Addiction and Mental Health realized that it was using a lot more resources than it should for its operation. Specifically, the association was using more space and equipment, computers, than what is thought to be ideal. It wanted to optimize employee space utilization in its offices and reduce unnecessary overhead in the process.

A structured time study process that directly observes and measures human activity in the rooms and usage of computers is an option, but its results are highly variable and inconclusive.

GGZ sought the help of 30mhz to address its problems. 30mhz installed 160 PIR (passive infrared) and vibration sensors to measure the occupancy for its over 100 rooms and over 1,500 desktop computers. The data were fed to an in-house analytics platform that enabled them to analyze peak times and average use.

From the results, the association was able to create a flexible room policy that optimized room use. It also determined the right number of computers they need for their business operation. As a result, GGZ generated savings in the overhead of €525,000 from its efficiency improvement and reduction in excess capacity for its rooms and desktop computers. It achieved a 10% reduction in its desktops and an impressive 650% return on its investment.

Expert Analysis by Piyanka Jain

Author of *Behind Every Good Decision,* and President & CEO of Aryng

This is a very cool example of utilizing IoT to solve a pervasive problem of underutilization of resources. The company started with the end in mind, always a must when problem-solving. The question was—We are using too many computers and too much space. Can we reduce it? They then used a systematic approach to utilize millions of spatial and movement data points to size the issue and propose reducing space and computers towards significant savings. However, given the narrative and just a 10% reduction in computers, I wonder if they laid out the hypotheses before delving into sensor data. They might find even more savings if they think through potential underutilization areas as they frame the problem. For example—if there are certain times where utilization is still less than 50%, then a scheduler might lead to even more significant savings.

In the future, GGZ can start thinking about potentially utilizing these sensors for improving other areas of operations like improving patient wait time, setting up security, and other alerts, if they are not already. They can also utilize the hypothesis-based approach of problem-solving to find the most significant cost-saving areas and start addressing those areas one-by-one in order of priority. Perhaps there are even more significant savings to be capitalized on.

28: Crowdsourcing Data Enrichment When Technology Fails

#usa #northamerica #software #architecture #engineering
#construction #media #entertainment #manufacturing
#AI #crowdsourcing #sales #reporting #document

Autodesk is a global leader in design that makes software for architecture, engineering, construction, media and entertainment, and manufacturing industries. Its software and services harness emerging technologies such as 3D printing, AI, generative design, and robotics, enabling companies and individuals to effectively work throughout the entire project lifecycle. Its main products include AutoCAD, BIM360, Civil 3D, Fusion 360, InfraWorks, and Inventor. Autodesk's total subscriber base has grown to almost 5 million users.

To identify its most promising sales leads and incentivize its sales team to pursue them, Autodesk needed to have complete data on every lead, such as company industry, size, and parent company. However, its database of customer information, which comes from different sources, is unreliable. The data are often either incomplete or the information is inaccurate. There is a need to integrate them into a single, reliable data source.

Traditional data vendors could provide data enrichment for only 70% of Autodesk's database, which was not good enough for the company to be able to implement its new sales strategy. The company started to incentivize its salespeople based on the industry of the customer. This would mean that 30% of Autodesk's salespeople will not get properly incentivized.

The Autodesk in-house team that started to work on the task employing some manual processes did not offer scalability and permanent structure, so crowdsourcing became an option.

Crowdflower (now part of Appen) was selected for its service and product. The supplier built a solution that is based on its proprietary business workflow. It leverages a pool consisting of millions of human contributors that research companies on demand. Information from multiple contributors is cross-checked and integrated into a single set of data before being sent back to Autodesk. In its initial implementation, CrowdFlower processed nearly a half million records for Autodesk.

Unlike the option with legacy data providers that charge annual licensing fees, Autodesk purchases and retains data from CrowdFlower rather than licensing it; Autodesk owns their data.

With the crowdsourcing service, the percentage of customer records with complete information improved from 70% to 85%. More complete and quality data translates into more sales leads data and incentivizes the sales team to pursue. Furthermore, there annual data licensing fees normally paid to legacy data providers have been significantly reduced.

Expert Analysis by Sunil Soares

CEO at YourDataConnect, LLC

This is a great use case for data monetization at scale. Autodesk reduced costs by pivoting away from traditional data providers as well as the use of expensive inhouse resources for data augmentation. At the same time, Autodesk potentially increased revenues by releasing more qualified leads to the sales team.

Autodesk also used a non-traditional approach to data stewardship by engaging legions of Crowdflower's contributors to improve the quality of lead data. Autodesk did this in a cost-effective manner by not bringing on these resources on to its payroll.

29: A Custom Solution to a Stock Problem

#uk #europe #middleeast #fashion #clothing #datadriven #forecasting #digitaltransformation #datascience #ai #automation #advancedanalytics #predictive #product #customer #retail

River Island is a London-based private company that designs, distributes, and retails high street fashion brand women's, men's, and children's clothing, footwear, and accessories. With 350 stores in the UK, it operates in many worldwide markets including Ireland, Russia, Poland, and other countries in Europe and the Middle East. It also conducts business through six online websites operating in four currencies and shipping to over 100 countries worldwide.

The company realized that it must keep up with the evolving customer demands and be at the forefront of innovation if it hopes to maintain its leadership position in the industry. It also felt it had to find a way to increase sales, improve sell-through and increase profitability.

The challenge was for the company to become agile and data-driven to be able to provide great customer experiences and empower their teams. It hoped to bring about the needed changes to anticipate quick-shifting customer demands, improve the efficiency of their forecasting and inventory management decisions at SKU/store granularity level, and increase product availability while maintaining healthy coverage levels across their network.

River Island chose Nextail as their technology partner because they have a shared agile retail philosophy. Nextail implemented true digital transformation that required ingraining data science and technology into the core of the River Island business to increase efficiencies and provide a seamless customer experience across channels.

AI automation and advanced analytics enable River Island to leverage predictive demand forecasting. Now they can quickly and efficiently prioritize stock across channels for allocation and replenishment based on where they have a higher likelihood of being sold.

Automated, data-driven merchandising decisions through Nextail lowered stockouts and fewer lost sales. River Island's stock outs dropped by 23.7% for continuity products and 10.9% for fast fashion products, while maintaining healthy coverage levels. Additionally, a 28.3% and 14.8% drop in lost sales for continuity products and fast fashion products respectively were achieved.

As a result, River Island has been able to increase sales and achieve better sell-out ratios.

River Island achieved organizational efficiencies by automating processes and decision-making. With clearer, more aligned efforts across teams and roles, the company has gained more efficient decision-making and team agility. Unique smart reports have helped merchandisers gain more time to carry out strategic planning and new tasks that can contribute to even more improvements to the business.

Expert Analysis by Jay Zaidi

Founder and Managing Partner, AlyData

Like every other organization, River Island has rightly decided to transform digitally to drive better business outcomes—better customer experience, improved customer intimacy, increase employee productivity etc. Their decision to focus on improving their business value chain (orders through delivery) is the key to success, since it delivers value to customers and ensures that they're able to reduce stock outs and improve coverage levels.

In my experience, small and mid-sized firms tend to be mired in legacy systems and tend to accumulate technology and data debt. In this case, it seems to me that River Island was able to overcome these challenges and utilize Nextail's capabilities to deliver outsized business outcomes.

The case study indicates that River Island achieved organizational efficiencies by automating processes and decision-making, which is significant. It did this by clearer, more aligned efforts across teams and roles, the company has gained more efficient decision-making and team agility. In addition, it implemented Smart Reports to improve decision making. What this tells me is that they focused on and successfully deployed all aspects of their data program—people (roles/responsibilities/accountability), process (automation/repeatability), technology (Nextail/et al) and tools (Smart Reports etc.). Highlights the fact that data programs are multi-dimensional in nature and hence require management's buy-in and support for investments in people, processes, technology and tooling to be successful.

The challenges they might have had or overcome include:

- *Becoming data-driven and evidence-based requires buy-in from the top—since it involves significant investment in people, process, technology, tools, and training. I'm sure one or more* leaders at River Island had to make the case for this and push for sponsorship.

- I'm assuming that the firm may not be very mature in its data management and governance practices and most likely had to initiate a maturity program to overcome challenges.

- Introducing new tools, terminology, processes and technology is a change management challenge. River Island would have had to focus on managing change throughout this journey, to ensure that all the key players were onboard and embraced the changes being introduced across the firm.

Going forward, it seems like the first set of objectives were focused around increasing sales and achieving better sell-out ratios. The firm may want to focus next on upsell and cross-sell opportunities based on insights related to customers' buying and browsing behavior and utilizing its omni-channel presence to drive personalization and targeted marketing campaigns. Fashion retail is a very competitive field with disruptive players such as H&M, Uniqlo and Zara creating new business models and significantly changing how business is done. River Island should certainly take some pointers from its competition and utilize its new and improved data-driven insights and inventory management capabilities to adjust its business model too.

30: SPEEDING-UP HIGH-SPEED RAIL MAINTENANCE

#italy #europe #transport #travel #locomotives #iot #sensors #monitoring #realtimedata #predictive #digitaltransformation #rail

TrenItalia is the leading train transport operator in Italy. Its fleet of 32,500 trains, carriages, and locomotives carry about 2 million passengers every day traveling over 250 million km per year. Its newest flagship train, the ETR 1000, can travel at speeds of up to 360 km/hr (220 mph) and carry 600 passengers.

TrenItalia is comprised of several business units such as Long-Distance Passenger Transport, Commuter Traffic, and Freight Service that serve customers at national and international levels.

The old system of maintenance does not bode well with the needs of the modern TrenItalia train system. It relied on the number of kilometers traveled or the amount of time that passed since the last maintenance service to determine when to perform maintenance on the train. The company's high-speed trains require that all their parts and systems operate efficiently to cope with the trains' performance. A rail service maintenance process that is quick, efficient, and able to react quickly to operational stressors was needed.

TrenItalia worked with SAP to design and implement a "Dynamic Maintenance System" powered by SAP HANA. Millions of IoT sensors were installed on their fleet to collect data such as temperature, pressure, electrical signals, vibration, and many other characteristics in real-time. These sensors onboard send 5,000 signals per train every second.

The constant streams of enormous data are fed through on-board concentrators directly to the SAP HANA digital core. Real-time data is instantly and continuously analyzed. The system performs dynamic planning via algorithmic predictions and indicators. More data that is collected makes the system smarter.

SAP HANA uses predictive analytics to anticipate failures before they occur. It guides TrenItalia when and what type of maintenance is needed to be performed. TrenItalia's IoT digital transformation translated to an 8 to 10% savings on its €1.3 billion annual maintenance cost. This new digital approach provided TrenItalia customers the fastest service in the business, highest reliability, and on-time scheduling that they desire. Moreover, the 700 TB of data processed per year through SAP HANA and SAP IQ results in better error forecasting, improved asset reliability, and service.

Expert Analysis by Neil Raden

CEO & Principal Analyst at Hired Brains Research
and Co-Author of *Smart (Enough) Systems*

An earlier effort using IoT sensor data for proactive maintenance was for oil field maintenance. It worked very well, altering the organization that conditions were ripe for disruption in a well, which is very costly. When an alert pops up, a field engineer would be dispatched to keep it online, but the problem was the system was not very smart about optimizing resources, and the field maintenance organization wasn't equipped for real-time alerts (or false positives). It would send an engineer to a remote well, then another one 100 miles away the next day, and the next day, another problem within two miles of the first well.

Nevertheless, it was very effective and has been enhanced and expanded with success. The TrenItalia application is clearly vital for the railroad, both for managing maintenance costs as well as downtime and real-time sensor activity has been shown in other rail operations to avoid disruptive failures as well as catastrophic accidents. So, despite being a business-oriented application, it also has the element of providing safety in a social context. But like the oilfield application, it takes more than the technology solution—the maintenance organization has to be aligned and equipped to perform effectively. This is true of most AI applications: they exist in a field of other applications and processes, they don't standalone to work their magic.

31: MAKING SALES FORECASTS POP

#usa #northamerica #food #beverage #nutrition #retail
#datawrangling #dataforecasting #predictive #document #analytics

PepsiCo, Inc, is a multinational food and beverage company whose products are widely known and consumed by users throughout the world. Headquartered in Purchase, New York, the company ranks as one of the top companies with the highest market value worldwide.

PepsiCo products are enjoyed by consumers one billion times a day in more than 200 countries and territories around the world. PepsiCo's billions of dollars of revenue are driven by a complementary food and beverage portfolio that includes Frito-Lay, Gatorade, Pepsi-Cola, Quaker, and Tropicana among others. PepsiCo's product portfolio includes a wide range of enjoyable foods and beverages, including 22 brands that generate more than $1 billion each in estimated annual retail sales.

The success of PepsiCo is anchored on accurately calculated sales forecasts. The company's analysts create intelligent forecasts by constantly comparing sales results against predictions for their huge retailers. Through this approach, the company will be able to drive inventory and production plans efficiently.

The challenge, however, lies in analyzing performance sales for more than 10 retailers, requiring each of the company's analysts to manually create and update 4 to 5 reports weekly. To add to the problem, these Analysts only utilized MS Excel and Access tools, which are slow, tedious, and prone to errors.

To overcome these challenges, PepsiCo partnered with Trifacta, a privately-owned software company based in San Francisco, but with satellite offices in Boston, London, and Berlin. Trifacta provides software designed to help individuals and companies efficiently use, explore, and transform data for smart analysis. By using Trifacta's data wrangling system, PepsiCo's retailers' data and reports were analyzed at an organizational scale fast, efficiently, and accurately. The company used Trifacta as a centralized solution in making data forecasts.

"Trifacta brought an entirely new level of productivity to the way our analyst and IT teams explore diverse data and define analytic requirements. Our users can intuitively and collabora-tively prepare the growing variety of data that makes up PepsiCo's analytic initiatives," Ben Sokol, Data Integration Analyst of PepsiCo, shared.

As a result, the reporting time of PepsiCo's analysts was reduced by 70% and their report generation time has been reduced to as much as 90% compared to the traditional manual method. Additionally, the responses to sales trends become readily available, saving costs, and preventing wastage.

Expert Analysis by Ranjana Young

Global Head of Enterprise Data and Analytics at Cardinal Health

This story clearly highlights the power of having data available to the analysts for them to analyze trends and the forecasting results versus spending days and weeks wrangling data from various sources. Trifacta took a 4-pronged approach:

- *Leverage technology to integrate and centralize several sources of data to automate report generation and provisioning, this clearly reduced the time to market*

- *Work with sales team to outline what diverse data sets are required so their analysis is much more predictive and prescriptive versus descriptive to really understand how analytics can drive better forecasting*

- *Integrate diverse data sets with the traditional sources to produce analytics that are more predictive and prescriptive*

- *Deliver the insights produced so the sales teams are taking actions based on the insights*

The technology clearly played a role in having the right platform as well as the tools that helped Trifacta integrate the many sources of data, acquire diverse data sets and automate the delivery of reports and insights. Additionally, it is clear that the collaboration between technology, data and the sales teams helped in creating process efficiency and removing waste.

32: ENABLING REAL-TIME ANALYTICS IS NO GAME

#scotland #europe #gaming #videogames #predictive #analytics
#customer #mobile #entertainment #behavior #retention

DeltaDNA is a name that is popular in the gaming industry for its real-time analytics and innovative marketing solutions. Game creators and developers throughout the world partner with this Scotland-based firm for its superior performance, flexible environment, and market-leading deep data functionality that drive maximum player engagement and determine user's lifetime value through intelligent player segmentation, targeted interventions, and predictive modeling.

While mobile and online gaming is here to stay — and continue to capture the hearts and attention of consumers worldwide — one of the biggest challenges that game developers face is converting free-to-play customers into paying ones. To do this, engagement plays a key role. First, developers must attract players with free gaming experiences, gain their trust and confidence, and then finally convert them to become engaged and loyal players. By boosting player engagement, game creators and developers will be able to improve player retention and increase profit.

To help game developers achieve this goal, deltaDNA partnered with Vertica Systems, an analytics database management software company based in Massachusetts, USA. By using the Vertica software, the analytics engine of the Haven Big Data Platform, deltaDNA was able to offer a smart and sophisticated player analytics application to game developers, enabling them to understand players' behaviors and respond to them in near real-time—crucial information to game developers.

As a result, deltaDNA was able to analyze and respond to players' behaviors within milliseconds, even across huge data sets. The system processes 99.9% of messages within 200 milliseconds, which means easily identifying if a game is frustratingly difficult or a challenge is overly confusing, or a player is easily bored. Through these valuable insights, developers can then create interventions to change the players' experience or response to any game, re-engaging them before they decide to quit the game.

As a result, player engagement increased to 350%, while player retention boosts revenue by as much as 6 times. Additionally, replacing the traditional sluggish analytics processes with a modern, more intelligent capability reduced game development cycles by 2 weeks.

With the analytics solution deltaDNA built, gaming companies have become more confident in investing in online and mobile games and acquired a higher level of trust in their revenue projections. For them, developing and launching games have become smoother and less risky.

Expert Analysis by Peter Aiken

Associate Professor of Information Systems at Virginia Commonwealth University, and current president of DAMA International

While the focus of this exercise is on the behavior of the players interacting with the game, I think that even greater impact could come from incorporating externally verified player demographic information. So much is tied up in role playing these days, it is now critical to understand whether the player typically adopts one or more personas so that the player behavior can be evaluated in context.

While the results indicate increase engagement—this is only mentioned as "retention boosts revenue." Likely deltaDNA will need to also take a step back from the instantaneous analyses to include analysis of longer-term trends—a sort of Thinking Fast Thinking Slow (Kahneman) approach. I am certain that there are lessons from the telco industry efforts at customer retention and conversation that can be incorporated here.

33: WEATHER OR NOT TO SERVE UP ADS

#usa #northamerica #global #weather #forecasting
#customer #monitoring #smartdata

Every day, more than 1.5 billion people worldwide rely on AccuWeather for weather news, updates, and forecasts. With the real-time weather information that the company provides, people can maximize their day, protect their businesses, and plan their indoor and outdoor activities accordingly. AccuWeather brings up-to-the-minute weather forecasts on computers, smartphones, tablets, television, radio, and newspapers around the world.

With a monthly average of 500 million visitors on desktop and mobile web, AccuWeather provides multiple ad spaces on their website where advertisers can promote and market their brand, products, or services to millions of people worldwide, enabling them to boost their sales and revenue on the AccuWeather website.

Aside from a simple placement on the website, AccuWeather wanted to provide additional value to their advertisers. Steve Mummey, Director of Ad Strategy & Audience Development of

AccuWeather, wanted to better understand the behavior and interests of their visitors so that they can display relevant ads and ideal messaging from their ad partners. To achieve this, AccuWeather integrated its DoubleClick for Publishers (DFP) account with Google Analytics 360.

AccuWeather uses DoubleClick for Publishers to serve and manage ads across its website. On the other hand, it uses Google Analytics 360 to help identify and understand the behaviors of website visitors. Before integrating the systems, there was no clear alignment between the ads and users' interests. For instance, a female user who is an active online shopper would see ads that are about sports or online gaming. Naturally, ad partners would not acquire clicks and conversions from this type of ad publishing, negatively affecting their revenues.

However, when the AccuWeather integrated data across these systems, it began getting smarter data and more valuable insights, enabling them to ideally match the ads being displayed on the website to the type of user currently visiting particular web pages. For example, visitors who love to travel are now being served with ads about flights, hotel accommodations, tour packages, and other related products and services.

Having the capability to acquire valuable insights like this, AccuWeather has been able to craft advertising packages that are highly tailored and customized for high-value unique audience segments, enabling its sales teams to sell fast and effectively. This perfect combination of DoubleClick for Publishers and Google Analytics 360 has not only provided AccuWeather with a deeper understanding of their website visitors but also enabled them to display relevant ads matching their visitors' needs and interests.

The integration has given users a better experience while increasing AccuWeather's revenue per session by 45%.

Expert Analysis by Della Shea

VP Privacy & Data Governance CPO at Symcor Inc

This case study is neither flashy nor revelatory by today's standards. At first glance the reader will say "big deal—match activity to ads—that is so 2010." Plus this model is symbolic of the much maligned "surveillance capitalism" model. While this cased is now considered typical, it doesn't mean we can't get anything from it.

Let's look deeper. There are two lessons here.

1. *Focusing on matching content to consumers. This is something any organization can appreciate. Showing ads is now tolerated to some degree or are even ignored. To get to the next level, the data needs to work for the consumer as well as a source of ad revenue. Lots of people use AccuWeather. Lots of people see the ads. But do they actually work for anyone? This is the vital next step for any organization that depends on internet generating some sort of revenue. Much like DVRs and hitting SKIP on the YouTube video—consumers will ignore ads unless they can connect.*

2. *The "secret sauce" in this case is integration of the data products. Note that greater value was not achieved until some data integration occurred. It highlights that the "best-of-breed" approach for any data products is not enough. IT will require some additional bespoke actions before full value is extracted.*

The view of this sort of case study is different now than 5 years ago, and going forward requires some fresh thinking. Privacy and ethics play a bigger role. The tolerance for irrelevant ads has always declined, regardless of the medium. Remember that cable TV rose to fame because you could pay for content, without the commercials. How well did that work out?

AccuWeather should to stay clear of the "surveillance capitalism" mantra. They need to:

1. highlight and increase the value of the experience or they will see declining use as people begin to want more for "their" data, or find alternate sources. For example, US government has many web sites with weather dat. Not as flashy, but just as informative.

2. visit growing trends in data ethics—changes in what "people want to know that you know" could create some serious pressure on their model.

3. keep abreast of privacy regulations. As of this writing, GDPR, CCPA and many other regulatory items are heading out into industry.

If ad restriction happens, then they need to go back to content. Enhance the actual experience. This is where they can also apply analytics—what types of pages work, which ones do not? At the end of the day, it is all about content that works. Point analytics at that area. The ads will take care of themselves.

34: A Beacon of Hope for Increased In-Store Revenue

#usa #northamerica #bluetooth #software #smartphone
#smartdevice #location #sensor #analytics #recommendation

I Beacon is a smart and modern technology developed by Apple. Based on Bluetooth Low Energy (BLE), iBeacon is natively built into Apple's operating system and devices, and serves as an indoor positioning system. Through this advanced functionality, businesses can advertise their presence to nearby users who are using smart devices. With iBeacons set up, companies, stores, and businesses can send promotional messages to potential customers when they walk past an iBeacon.

A major omnichannel retailer wanted to gain visibility on customers' path inside their store to be able to enhance customer experience and boost their revenue. They understand that the store layout and placement of products and merchandise can somehow affect their sales.

While in-store sensors, QR codes, and RFID tags can help address this concern, the data formats generated by these tools and technologies are incompatible with the company's legacy systems. Thus, the company looked for better alternatives and discovered Apple's iBeacon technology.

As the company started testing iBeacon in its flagship store, the tool began capturing location data of shoppers who are using iPhones and Android devices inside the store. Each data is unified into big data, revealing the way customers move around the retail shop. With this valuable information, the company was able to compare customers' movements with the location of specific products. As the iBeacon program grows and more and more data are being collected, it enables the company to process a huge volume of sensor and micro-location data.

The retailer's big data analytics system using iBeacon played a vital role in reorganizing product placements and optimizing in-store experience, which in turn, increased store sales by 10%. Furthermore, the tool contributed to the reduction of unnecessary inventory and enhancement of customer satisfaction through smarter product placement and a more intuitive store layout.

Expert Analysis by Robert (Bob) S. Seiner

President and Principal at KIK Consulting & Educational Services, Publisher of *The Data Administration Newsletter*

There are already regular occurrences of merely mentioning or searching for something that result in being inundated by advertisements from companies selling these types of products or services. These advertisements "magically" appear through social media and other interactive devices. It is not magic; it is the use of modern data technology. Beacons, or by definition—guiding lights that are dependent on behavior—already exist and they already impact the products and services we learn about and therefore purchase. Until now, the invasive nature of this type of promotion has been reserved for contact through social media—and not our daily visits to the grocery or big box stores.

Interestingly, the iBeacon technology assists the retailers and the customers in other ways as well. Bigger stores arrange the merchandise in their stores according to how people maneuver through the stores. Retailers position products, together and apart, to increase the possibility that you will purchase more items. Retailers track what is being purchased together and place products accordingly targeted at maximizing their sales. Products are put on sale, while the prices of other products that are regularly purchased at the same time are increased even slightly, to make up the margins. Positioning means everything to the retailers, and iBeacons allow the retailers to know how people navigate through the stores, and they position products accordingly.

By stating that the iBeacon product improves the customer experience, and retailer's sales, and by not considering privacy or customer interaction concerns, the case study appears to bring in only one side of the discussion. Is this something customers want? How will the customers gain from this "improved customer experience"?

Customers already "sell" their data to the retailers by using the frequent shopper cards and by shopping on-line. Most customers accept the discounts that are provided via the cards, while at the same time know that they are providing their data associated with each sale—what was purchased, how often, what time of day, what was purchased with what, and so on. Customer are used to opting in to provide data in return for lower prices. The question is, will the customers be willing to be notified about products and services throughout a store when physically visiting the retail locations?

The next question is, if customers are willing to provide information about where they are in the store, how they are navigating through the store, along with the products they are purchasing, where does this data interaction end?

Other uses of this positioning technology potentially include:

- *The entertainment industry, with theme parks, educational facilities like museums, even your local establishments like shopping districts, malls, and other places that people visit often to track how people navigate and message potential customers.*

- *City planners, could track people's movement through the streets, know where they stop, park, visit and purchase goods or service, to message them about attractions and businesses.*

- *Transportation hubs like airports and train stations could leverage these beacons to track the movement and activities of customers and potential customers.*

- *Places of business could utilize this technology to track employees and visitors.*

- *Virtually any place could utilize this technology to gather information from people without their knowing it for acceptable or unacceptable reasons.*

The use of iBeacons in large retailers may just be the start. Keep your eyes out for advanced and additional uses of this technology in the future.

35: Showing How to Increase Click-Through Rate

#india #asia #entertainment #movie #concert #sports #event
#ticketing #clicks #tracking #analytics #customer #transaction

BookMyShow is India's largest online entertainment ticketing hub, selling more than 10 million tickets monthly. BookMyShow enables users to book and purchase tickets for movies, concerts, sports, plays, and live events through its online platform, mobile website, and mobile app. Aside from these, the website also features show times and schedules, trailers, movie reviews, and upcoming events near you. It also provides promotional offers and discount coupons to loyal customers.

Although the company was getting good traction on its main website, improving the click-through rate (CTR) on the mobile site was the primary focus. They wanted to ensure that users of the mobile site were not only enjoying their content but also pushing through to make a booking and completing their transactions.

To fulfill this goal. BookMyShow had to put specific data-driven tracking tools in place. The company was able to accurately collect required data using a comprehensive tracking system, which helped them understand user behavior better and more efficiently. The analytics team also strategized how to take advantage of custom marketing funnels to help them properly identify the stage at which users drop off during a booking process. True enough, upon implementing funnel tracking and data analysis, they were not only able to understand the page-level behavior of users, but they also found ways to prevent them from leaving the site.

This integrated solution resulted in an increase of 55% in click-through rate and a 6% increase in conversion rate. Because of this, BookMyShow continues to dominate the online entertainment ticketing industry in India.

Expert Analysis by Ramesh Dontha

Managing Partner at Digital Transformation Pro, Best Selling Author, and Global Top 250 Podcast Host in Tech

The case study highlights 3 most important aspects of a customer journey on web & mobile apps: (1) customer initiation (2) customer intent (3) customer conversion. For customer initiation, BookMyShow rightfully prioritized mobile app given that the majority of the customers are using mobile devices. Given that Google Analytics can only track some aspects of customer journey such as source, CTR, bounce rate, the company filled the gaps with respect to conversion rate optimization and cross-sell/upsell optimization during customer exits.

In the future, BookMyShow can possibly keep the customers on their websites and mobile apps for a longer duration by providing entertainment videos such as movie trailers or celebrity exclusive

content. The company can then monetize with advertisements or sponsorships. Additionally, the company can also work with extended ecosystem partners such as Uber/Lyft (for transportation to events) or hotels & restaurants with the exit funnels which are already in place.

36: EXTREME DIGITAL MARKETING

#usa #northamerica #marketing #adstrategy #seo
#media #consumer #datadriven #predictive #modeling
#advancedanalytics #marketing #customer

DX Marketing (DXM) *specializes* in utilizing consumer data to create business strategies and provide a quantifiable ROI on marketing spend. The company focuses on building data-driven digital marketing to its clients by offering a comprehensive suite of digital products specifically designed to improve, boost, and optimize various marketing accountabilities, including audience segmentation, market analysis, customer acquisition, engagement, retention, and achieving ROI.

For DXM, data is essential to everything they do. Their products are designed to collect and analyze data for clients and then leverage the insights into predictive models that will help the clients achieve their specific end goals. This includes analyzing audience behavior in different channels, converting website visits into sales, entering a new geographic market, maximizing ROI, or a combination of all of the above. With so many data sources available, the company needed a big data and advanced analytics platform to manage and identify valuable consumer data and unify their hundreds of millions of records.

As it turned out, the solution to DXM's data problems is a set of products integrated to work seamlessly and more efficiently together. The company utilized a combination of Oracle Autonomous Data Warehouse, Oracle Advanced Analytics, and Oracle Marketing Cloud.

First, the data warehouse consolidated the multiple data sources of DXM, functioning as a smart repository for DXM's many data sources, including the demographic data and updates from Epsilon that regularly come in every six weeks. And a predictive modeling application made it easy for DXM users to create in-depth marketing reports and develop valuable insights without the need for technical knowledge or assistance from an IT expert or data scientist.

By combining these powerful and intuitive analytics tools into a single data machine, DXM witnessed significant improvements on all levels. The company was able to leverage more than a terabyte of data consisting of 115 million households, with 260 million individuals within those households and roughly 800 attributes for each record. Furthermore, the system helped decrease customer acquisition cost by 52%, increase delivery speed by 70%, and boost revenues by 25% in the first six months after deployment.

Expert Analysis by Jason Krantz

CEO & Founder of Strategy Titan

Being able to tie D&A investments to improved financial performance is one of the most common strategic misses I see. Having a clear path from investment to financial improvement separates the "nice to have" initiatives from the "need to have." DXM made ROI a foundational part of their value proposition and focus. This helps provide a clean answer to the question "what am I getting (or will I get) out of this investment?"

DXM also implemented had a reliable process to sort through all their available data and deliver the content of interest to customers, and then they made it even better. Many firms will deliver a lot of data to customers and leave it to them to sort through it. For many organizations sorting through that information to find the content of interest and value is hard.

Removing this intermediate step and presenting the information in a relevant and cohesive manner shortens the time to insights for customers and adds a significant amount of value for DXM's customers.

Considering the vast cache of data DXM has, it is likely that they have growth opportunities in a wide number of industries. One strategy to help accelerate that growth is to partner with other organizations that already have a strong presence in industries and channels of interest.

One way this idea could unfold: DXM can serve as a data provider while their partners offer services that help their customers better leverage the data. Revenue share could be a very appealing proposition here and could benefit everyone involved.

New customers can get data they might not normally use, new customers will have a partner to help them make the most of their investment, channel partners have a new offering to bring their customers, and DXM gains access to new markets and channels that were under penetrated before. The result for DXM is more revenue and quicker expansion into desired industries and channels.

37: Sifting for Payment Fraud

#usa #northamerica #digitalmarketplace #ecommerce
#selling #machinelearning #product #customer
#automation #fraud #monitoring #alerting #AI

Wanelo *is a digital marketplace* where consumers can discover and buy products from the internet. It has over 550,000 stores in its site which include big-name brands as well as little-known tiny independent boutiques selling 30 million products. 90% of its users come from the US but the company maintains marketplace remote support teams globally.

The company started as a social shopping site and eventually evolved as a marketplace with mobile-focused merchants, growing its sellers 5x since its inception. It targets mainly Gen Z consumers. It has 11 million users, predominantly female. 85% of Wanelo's traffic is from mobile devices.

Since they transformed into a marketplace, payment fraud became a concern. The chargeback rate increased to 0.87% including friendly fraud, which is seemingly legitimate and coming from good and valuable customers. Almost 70% of the chargebacks could be attributed to friendly fraud.

The Marketplace Operations team executes all manual order review and order disputes, including fraud cases. They needed an effective solution to the payment fraud they were encountering.

They applied the machine learning solution of Sift to the new challenge they face. Sift has helped them previously in weeding out the social space they were creating of spammers. This time, the Wanelo Team adopted the Sift Formulas feature of the automation tool as the foundation for their fraud prevention system. Being an existing Sift user, they asked the assistance of Sift with setting the system up for their particular business needs. The Sift engineers integrated the necessary additional APIs to be able to connect Sift Formulas with the internal order management system of the company. Their label history was likewise overhauled, which immediately brought useful and reliable Sift Scores.

Wanelo uses Sift Formulas daily. Having started with no experience in fraud management, with Sift, the fraud prevention team now can create and manage automation without the need for costly engineering resources. Wanelo identifies and responds to new patterns of suspicious behavior using Sift, which empowers them to immediately update their automation flow.

Dispute rates dramatically dropped by 77% and are currently down to around 0.20%. Likewise, an estimated 100–150 hours from the manual review are saved monthly. Wanelo is now able not only to simply react to fraud but can now take a proactive preventive approach, creating better efficiencies for its business.

Expert Analysis by Bill Schmarzo

Customer Advocate, Data Management Incubation, Dell Technologies

It's critically important to start with a well-defined business problem (like Fraud) that can deliver almost immediate material and demonstrable business benefits. And be sure to thoroughly vet the metrics and KPI's against which progress, and success will be measured with the key business stakeholders (to make sure that you are solving the right problems).

Since Wanelo depended upon a third-party vendor to provide the solution, Wanelo management needs to understand how the learnings from the application of the fraud reduction model are going to be codified, shared and reused by other parts of the business. For example, are they able to create, share and reuse "fraud propensity scores" that can predict ahead of time what times of customers and/ or what types of promotions and/or what types of transactions and/ or what types of products being sold are at higher-than-normal risk of fraud? Can they reuse those propensity scores to recruit the right types of merchants, and target the right types of customers who have a lower likelihood of fraud?

My recommendation would be to build a data lake that not only provides a single instance of the organization's lowest granular data that can be shared across other use cases, but to also store the customer, vendor and product fraud propensity scores that can be re-used across other use cases.

38: City of the Big Shoulders Adopts Big Data Solution

#usa #northamerica #chicago #finance #commerce #industry #culture #education #technology #transportation #telecommunication #cdo #document #predictive #analytics #prescriptive #government

With a population of nearly 2.7 million people, Chicago is the third most populous city in the US. An international hub for finance, commerce, industry, culture, education, technology, transportation, and telecommunications, Chicago has one of the highest gross domestic products (GDP) of any city in the world. Its economy is also one of the most developed and balanced in the world. It is the US city with the second greatest number of domestic and international visitors, after New York.

The population of the city and the number of economic activities make for Chicago's complexity that creates a great challenge to city managers. The city has 15 crucial services departments, including police, transportation, fire, public works, and sanitation. The value of tons of data coming from the different areas of city services is not fully realized as it is squirreled away in the city's siloed systems.

The City mayor wanted to have a geospatial platform linking all the municipal data in real-time, which can then be analyzed and acted on. Brett Goldstein, Chicago's Chief Data Officer was tasked to create a system fast that can develop entirely new real-time perspectives that the city could act on immediately to improve services.

Goldstein started with a single node of MongoDB and built it from there with his team. With MongoDB's powerful document storage, fast analytics, and scalable architecture, a real-time geospatial platform was made possible. The WindyGrid platform analyzes 7 million rows of data from different departments daily, can evolve schemas in real-time, and include predictive analytics from the data that constantly grows by the day.

With MongoDB, the city operations can now be captured into a unified view on a map of Chicago. The data can be analyzed, crucial insights can be derived, and new applications can be built. It gives city managers easy access to the entire city's spatial data, both historically and in real-time. Using analytics, they can determine the likely consequences of separate events such as faulty traffic lights and road emergencies, being able to address the problems before worse issues come up. They are also able to coordinate responses among the different departments and proactively put solutions in place in major events like the Chicago Marathon and serious snowstorms.

MongoDB WindyGrid created a central nervous system for Chicago that helps improve city services, save on costs, and create a more livable city.

Expert Analysis by William McKnight

President at McKnight Consulting Group

A municipality like Chicago has clearly defined services departments. A business may not have such clear organizational demarcations, but creating them for the project is important for establishing priorities, creating project milestones and dividing ownership.

Vendors love to take full credit and ROI for successful projects. However, it is unclear that other databases could not have been more effective (quicker to deploy, facilitating more function, lower costs and lasting longer without intervention) than the one chosen. The success of a project linking city-wide data is owed more to leadership, organization and process than it is to the database technology.

It was probably a good thing the CDO was asked to create a system fast. Quickness in delivering value is important to business and maintaining the enthusiasm of the development team. Business leaders need to support agile rollout and understand that what they see initially is not nearly the final product. Build teams need to communicate the rollout plan to the business leaders.

When there are millions of rows coming into a system daily, it is important to establish "tiers" in the architecture that are self-contained. An important one for this project would be the intake layer. The intake layer needs to self-report data received, processed, loaded, etc. because inevitably there will be delays and failures and the intake cannot completely fall behind. Users will need to be aware of the exact spot the intake process is at.

This system is very foundational for city functions over time. While it was built on the initial ROI to be delivered based on giving city managers access to data, they were able to add traffic light analysis, road emergency analysis and coordinated response uses of the data. This is a great example of acting locally by building for short-term wins and thinking globally by building the data layer—the most complex part of most projects—to support future projects.

39: DOWN UNDER UNIVERSITY BRINGS DOWN BUDGETING TIME AND EXPENSE

#australia #asiapacific #education #academia
#university #college #forecasting #selfservice
#reporting #budgeting #visualization #financial

The University of Adelaide is among the world's top 1% universities and a member of Australia's prestigious Group of Eight research-intensive universities. It has a rich history of excellence that spans 140 years. It has 4 campuses, with the main campus located in the heart of Adelaide.

The university boasts of being a destination of choice for highly talented researchers, students, and industry and government partners. Its student population totals 27,000, over 7,000 coming from more than 90 countries while its staff number 3,400. It also takes pride in counting among its distinguished alumni 5 Nobel Laureates and Australia's first female Prime Minister and Supreme Court judge.

The University of Adelaide had been having periods of year-on-year increases in student enrollment but when the number of students plateaued, the organization wanted to adjust its strategy. As a result, it embarked on a cost-efficiency improvement initiative to help them to obtain better value for students, researchers, and educators and attract students in a dynamic higher education sector. Also, pressure is increasing from the government for tertiary educational institutions to operate more like a business. The university had difficulty identifying the areas it needed to make changes because of limited insight into student enrollment and financials. Without clear visibility of how salaries, the biggest cost component, would change over time, the cost to the organization could not be determined and long-term forecasts could not be created. Also, the six months budget development process the organization used to have made budgeting difficult.

To solve the challenge, the University switched from its manual approach to reporting with an IBM Analytics solution utilizing on IBM Cognos Business Intelligence to standardize self-service and canned reporting and IBM Cognos TM1 software for performance management. With a single centralized solution that replaced multiple spreadsheets, the organization transformed its budgeting and forecasting approach, dramatically slashing the time and process involved and created unprecedented visibility of data for its managers. These solutions let managers recognize the most efficient departments and benchmark their effective measures elsewhere. And they can model fluctuating salary budgets to see the university's true operational costs for the first time.

This analytics implementation reduced the university's budget creation time for its departmental annual budgets by 50% to just 3 months. It also equipped the organization with clear visibility into the student body enabling financial staff to focus on improving student retention and other areas to build effective acquisition strategies.

Expert Analysis by Matthew B. Rager

Co-Founder and Managing Partner at West Monroe

Moving from a spreadsheet-based budgeting and forecasting process to a performance management solution adds transparency and agility in making business decisions. In the University of Adelaide's case, the ability to compare updated enrolment and salary data against budgets and forecasts allows them to target areas of inefficient spend or lower than expected enrolment.

Universities all over the world would have benefited from this type of agility as COVID-19 impacted enrolment and the need for remote learning. Being able to model changes to enrolment and tuition as well as changes to costs related to physical plant and staff for maintenance, housing, and food likely helped many universities in their strategies to adapt to a quickly changing world.

40: Conservation Efforts Grab Analytics by the Horn

#southafrica #africa #poaching #conservation #cloud #iot
#predictive #analytics #alerting #sensor #environment

South Africa has more than 70% of the world's total population of rhinoceros—about 20,000. A small percentage of the mammal species are in the surrounding African countries, particularly Zimbabwe and Namibia. Poaching of rhinos has been the greatest problem in the rhino conservation efforts. Poachers kill these animals for their horns, which have demands for usage especially in Asia.

MTN, a South-Africa based multinational mobile telecommunications company, and the Netherlands Research Institute (NRI) partnered to address and reduce the threats to the rhinos at South Africa's Welgevonden Game Reserve, a 135 sq. mile wildlife reserve. To do this, they harness the IBM cloud, IoT, and predictive analytics technologies.

Smaller animals that comingle with the rhinos, such as wildebeest, zebra, and antelope, which are easier to tag, are fitted with collars that can track the movement of these animals as they respond to the presence of human intruders. The sensors collect the animals' location, movement, speed, and direction, among other data. And they transmit data to by means of the long-range signal and control (LoRa) platform and a 3G network. IBM and NRI collaborated to create algorithms for animal behavioral analysis that serve as an early warning system. It alerts security personnel of dangerous situations, enabling them to act accordingly or deploy before any attack takes place.

This creative solution has been a great help in preserving the rhinos. It predicts imminent danger to the animals, particularly the threat posed by poachers moving through the area. In the first three years, this solution has resulted in a 15% decline in poaching, versus a 9000% increase in the seven years prior.

Expert Analysis by John Morris,

Data engineering evangelist and publisher of *Data Decisioning*.

There are so many marvelous aspects to South Africa's rhinoceros conservation program against illegal rhino poaching that it makes a perfect case study for any IoT and analytics program. From the start all analytics programs need a boundary; in this case the game reserve is an actual geographic boundary!

And analytics programs need domain knowledge: here zoology was the creative basis for the idea that park threat detection could be based on the behaviour of less-costly-to-tag herd animals than the more-costly-to-tag and less numerous rhinos.

Economics is an important factor behind this success story: the conservation program concerns a battle against persistent illicit demand, the cost of good data collection is a critical factor in systems design, and opportunity cost is very high when limited park staff respond to false alarms.

Interestingly, tracking and predicting the behaviour of herds of zebras in the wild is not unlike tracking and predicting the movements of crowds of people in our brave new smart cities! Beyond marvelous technology, any successful analytics program requires a strong foundation in law, ethics, domain behaviour—and economics too.

41: Data Monetization Is Thy Name (宝宝)

#china #asia #UK #europe #children #parents #recommendation
#automation #customer #lifestyle #innovation

For decades now, the Chinese couples have engaged in the practice of giving their children Western names to accompany their Chinese ones. This is intended for future potential opportunities for the children to study or do business in Western countries and other cross-cultural interactions. Chinese parents have tended to randomly choose Western names for their children. In part due to restrictions on access to or challenges understanding Western culture, sometimes children wind up with embarrassing or awkward names like Gandalf, Cinderella, or Rolex.

On one of her trips to China with her own parents, Beau Jessup, a 16-year-old girl from Gloucestershire, UK, was asked by local parents to suggest an English name to their Chinese baby. Beau decided to expand this idea by setting up a website called "Special Name" to help Chinese parents choose appropriate English names for their babies.

In local practice, the Chinese put a lot of emphasis on choosing names based on the five elements—fire, water, stone, metal, and wood. She developed an English baby-naming method similar to how they pick their Chinese names.

The website asks parents to provide their baby's gender and twelve desired personality traits for their children that will also reflect on the child's name. It will then match these traits and gender to a database of English names that have assigned personality traits. Three candidate names are shared on the WeChat social media platform, where family and friends can help make a final decision. After the name is chosen, the site generates a printable certificate with the name of the child, its meaning, and examples of famous people with that name.

In the first couple years, Beau Jessup's site helped name over 250,000 Chinese babies. The service charges a minimal fee but she has generated almost £50,000 (US$61,000), which she intends to use for her educational pursuits.

Expert Analysis by Benjamin Taub

Founder and CEO of Dataspace, and co-author
of three books on data warehousing

A sixteen-year-old figures out how to monetize data—Wow, what a kid!

A few things stand out to me here. First, is the value of collaboration. By allowing family and friends to contribute to the decision, Ms. Jessup has used the data she generates to build a collaborative environment, actually a crowdsourcing network with real consequence. If there's a "right" name, the wisdom of crowds, as James Surowiecki put it in his 2004 book, will likely choose it.

Second, this application plays to the fact that, despite global-ization, there are still great cultural differences around the world. Thus, one trick to global success is to commonize where possible to increase efficiencies yet customize where necessary to provide value.

Interestingly, this need for local customization could also provide an opportunity to expand this product globally. Now that Ms. Jessup is successfully serving China, could she tweak her algorithms and data to serve other markets? (So long as it doesn't interfere with her education, of course.)

42: It Doesn't Take Much Research to Share the Benefits of Shared Analytics

#usa #northamerica #health #medical #biotech #pharmaceutical #datascience #advancedanalytics #automation #predictive #prescriptive

I *QVIA is a leading industry player* in both clinical research and health information technology. With headquarters in Connecticut and North Carolina, it provides support services including contract research for clients in biotech, pharmaceutical, and medical fields.

IQVIA believes it needs more than data science to solve the biggest challenges in human health; it needs human data science. It aims to realize the potential of big data in healthcare and help customers address both current needs and future opportunities. The company is pursuing the seamless integration of unparalleled data, advanced analytics, transformative technology, and deep domain expertise.

IQVIA's highly manual business processes were saddled with inefficiencies and errors that prevent the company from being pro-active and innovative. Their technical capabilities were getting in the way of achieving their goal of advanced analytic capability and a higher level of analytic maturity.

The Global Financial Shared Services (GFSS) group took on the challenge to transform IQVIA's analytic capability and reduce cost across the organization. It implemented Alteryx Analytic Process Automation platform to easily share data and automate tedious and complex processes.

In the first year of utilizing Alteryx APA, $4.8M of benefit was realized. It is estimated that in the first three years, $28M in benefit will be achieved, resulting in a 30x ROI. As the platform use continues to expand across the business, IQVIA anticipates other benefits including reallocation of resources to lower-cost centers, identification of opportunities for early pay invoice discounts, and reduction of costs such as late fees due to slow approvals, costs related to compliance reporting, and consulting expenses.

The company was also able to free up significant capacity for more valuable work. Some of the benefits outside of the quantified ROI include 100% SOX compliance, scalability of analytics such as travel and expense reports to 6,500 managers, reduction of time spent on some tasks from 3–5 hours to minutes, analytics delivery daily rather than monthly, and measurement of KPI's that were impossible to track previously.

Expert Analysis by Cortnaye Swan

Director, Healthcare & Life Sciences at West
Monroe, Life Sciences Industry Leader

The most interesting thing about this story is that IQVIA is the leading data provider to the life sciences industry. Data is their business. They have monetized one of the largest and most comprehensive collections of healthcare information in the world, which includes more than one billion comprehensive, longitudinal, non-identified patient records spanning sales, prescription and promotional data, medical claims, electronic medical records, genomics, and social media.

They serve as a critical data intermediary to the healthcare ecosystem creating intelligent connections through analytics and transformative technology, yet they faced their own internal challenges in achieving advanced analytics maturity due to inefficient manual processes. This story reenforces the importance of analytic process automation technology in unlocking predictive and prescriptive insights that drive quantifiable ROI. Data alone is not enough; it takes a platform of tools and technology to extract value and insights from data.

43: INCREASED COUPON REDEMPTION REDEEMS INVESTMENT IN BIG DATA

#UK #europe #global #groceries #merchandise #retail
#petrol #banking #mobilephone #broadband #realtimeanalytics
#datalake #monitoring #predictive #forecasting #loyalty

Tesco is a British multinational groceries and general merchandise retailer. It is the third-largest retailer in the world and is the market leader of groceries in the UK, where it has a market share of around 28%, as well as in Ireland, Hungary, and Thailand. It has a total of 6,800 shops in 7 countries across Europe and Asia. Aside from supermarkets, Tesco also operates petrol stations, a bank, a mobile phone, home phone, and broadband businesses.

Tesco is a pioneer in technology and data. It is one of the first supermarket chains to initiate tracking customer activity through its loyalty card system, which started in 1995 it called Clubcard. The loyalty card, which currently has 16.5 million users, was not only for offering discounts but to generate valuable insights into the shopping behavior of their customers.

The company faces many challenges ranging from evolving customer behavior, the need to reduce wastage, and to square up to newer competitors. Tesco has over 3,000 stores in the UK alone. Each store stocks an average of 40,000 products. Tracking them all just once involves the creation of over 100 million data points.

Tesco's solution to these challenges is in cutting-edge, real-time analytics technology, and the most up-to-date data. The company outsources the data analysis to Dunnhumby, a company that specializes in data analysis, which they have utilized since the ClubCard started. From data warehousing, where the data was moved in batches for external analytics, the company moved to a data lake model, based around the Hadoop framework.

Using big data and predictive analytics through simulations, Tesco's analytics team observed historical sales and weather data to understand how the stock moved and will move through the company to optimize its stock-keeping system. They also processed tons of data coming in from the Clubcard to better target mailings of vouchers and coupons to customers.

More accurate forecasting and optimized store operations that they were able to implement resulted in a huge increase in the rate of coupon redemption—from 3% to 70%. Tesco was also able to save $152 million in stock that would have otherwise been expired and wasted.

Expert Analysis by Valerie Logan

Data literacy pioneer, CEO and Founder of The Data Lodge

Pioneers in their industry for over 100 years, few companies have such a lasting reputation as Tesco. This story of decades of innovation with data and analytics solutions, from early Clubcard bets that have paid off for customer behavior insights, to blending of external data before it was popular, to instrumentation of store sensors to optimize operations, Tesco has continually adapted and modernized their platform and developed specialized talent. And that adaptation has been a wild ride amidst shifting customer personas and behaviors (online ordering, delivery services, and pickup convenience), adjusting portfolio mix, and differentiating amidst a competitive landscape that Tesco could never have imagined back in the day.

Yes—modern tech, augmented processes and specialized talent with rock star data scientists and engineers are vital foundations and accelerators. But sustained success with data has to extend and reach beyond the specialists. The rest of the 450,000 employees are Tesco too—and are untapped participants in the data innovation, optimization and collaboration. They create the customer moments. They are walking sensors. They are front-line innovators. And their data literacy matters as an integral part of Tesco's pioneering legacy and future.

Intentional upskilling, engagement, culture hacks and interventions. Unlocking radical collaboration between data scientists and front-line associates. This is how Tesco will scale and hold its legendary position—by fostering a shared language and literacy around data for all associates. And if history is any indication of the future, Tesco is already all over it.

44: CHECKING CUSTOMER'S DATA TO STOP LOSING THEM

#usa #northamerica #global #payroll #humanresources #predictive #analytics #recommendation #customer #HR #employee

Paychex, Inc. is an American company that provides payroll and human resource outsourcing services that caters to small-to-medium-sized businesses. It has headquarters in Rochester, New York, and has more than 100 offices that serve about 670,000 payroll clients in the United States, Brazil, Germany, Denmark, Norway, and Sweden. Paychex has been named one of The World's Most Innovative Companies by Forbes, while Inc. voted has awarded Paychex Best HR Outsourcing Solution for Small Business.

However, Paychex had been losing about 20% of its customer base each year for various reasons. Not all small businesses find it easy to survive. Some opt-out for cost reasons and still, others are lost without the company knowing the real reasons. Losing a significant part of your customer base has far-reaching implications especially to the company's finances and the business as a whole. Paychex had to take immediate action. It wanted to have an accurate assessment of its customers' needs to correct the situation.

The company invested in predictive analytics to help. It developed a model that predicts high-risk customers. The tool can likewise track what the Paychex branches are doing or failing to do when it comes to increasing customer retention. The model was able to identify good practices by some branches. These branches developed a year-end retention program that targets clients who are most likely to leave, offering free payrolls and loyalty discounts to such customers. The analysis also helped the branches overcome their eagerness to unnecessarily offer discounts to all clients likely to stay with Paychex instead of targeting only those predicted by the model to be the most likely to leave. This type of call out significantly added to the bottom line.

The predictive tool also helps identify which of its payroll-only clients are the most likely to be interested in Paychex's 401(k) service business. The analytics routines consider a client's credit rating and payment history at Paychex and whether a client uses a competitor's services.

With the aid of analytics, the loss rate of Paychex customers dropped from 25.2% to just 6.7%. Also, with the use of its predictive tool, losses were cut by 50% when the retention team in one segment of the business proactively called them.

Expert Analysis by Wade Walker

Practitioner and executive consultant in data and analytics, and chair and organizer of the *DMC Intelligent Data Management Conference*

Paychex is an interesting case study in use of data science to surface subtle patterns and turn this into business value. In this case, predictive analytics of subtle customer behavior change, and probably financial indicators has identified an actionable opportunity for customer retention. Analysis of behavior over time, either as an organization or individual in my experience, is an excellent indicator of interests and engagement and potential future opportunity.

In the case study however, loss of 20% of Paychex's customer base year on year is a clear indicator that there are greater pains at play here, and the use of Predictive Analytics has only provided a lifeline upon which Paychex must act. Paychex likely needs to critically analyze its business model and product offerings to realign it with market demands. Once a new suite of services and service packages is launched, layering predictive and prescriptive (i.e., 'next best action or offer') on a sufficiently large training dataset could be expected to drive growth as Paychex's new business processes drive continuous improvement to align and evolve with customer expectations and needs.

To take this further, marrying physical event data (i.e., 'traditional' data) with Digital Body Language (data on customer behavior and engagement with an organization's Digital channels) provides a robust and well-rounded opportunity to innovate and deliver content of interest, increase engagement and drive long term retention and customer value. With a suite of services that aligns to market demand, insight and targeting provided by machine learning-informed activities and prescriptive analytics-driven CRM coupled with call centre activity focused on returning customer value, organizations such as Paychex can be expected to see measurable impact on long-term business potential.

45: Impatience with Lack of Data Insights Helps Patients

#usa #northamerica #healthcare #research #clinical
#datamining #predictive #analytics #modeling #customer
#patient #datawarehouse #ai #nonprofit

*C*ornerstone Research Institute, LLC is a $3B Orlando, Florida-based based multi-specialty group and research center serving for both inpatient and outpatient clinical trials. It has various services and facilities to support its clinical trials such as physical exams, routine blood draws, EKG, drug screens, urinalysis, MRI, X-ray as well as physician consultation. It has 19 staff that consists of physicians, study collaborators, and nurses. The research institute has different areas of focus including COPD, Crohn's, post-operative pain control, hot flashes, constipation, arthritis, and others.

In connection with its research services related to mental health, Cornerstone Research Institute conducts clinically relevant research for the benefit of patients with mental illness. They work with a network of more than 130 non-profit community health locations in Indiana and Tennessee in this area. There has been an increased demand for mental health services. On the other hand, Cornerstone, like most healthcare providers and non-profits, experiences funding cuts and lower reimbursement schedules. Despite these, it wants practice-based evidence to provide clinicians with relevant information to help improve patient outcomes.

Cornerstone used IBM SPSS to create a data-mining solution that leverages predictive analytics to analyze multi-variable patient treatment information to come up with individualized predictions of patient outcomes. Data from clinical databases, internal EHR, and patient interviews were integrated into sophisticated predictive models to analyze 14 variables from more than 9,000 patients. The variables include demographic and socioeconomic information and a range of diagnostic and clinical data. The predictive model analyzes the effectiveness of different medications and treatment modalities to determine the most beneficial for patients under various conditions.

The patient-generated data provided better insights to improve patient outcomes. The information is stored in a data warehouse to facilitate knowledge-sharing and best practices between thousands of healthcare providers and research professionals.

Currently, there are 400,000 patient records centralized in a single data warehouse which can scale up to 20 million records. They can be conveniently retrieved to aid clinicians in the effective treatment of mental health patients. With AI, a 42% improvement in patient outcomes is anticipated. Likewise, a 58% reduction in cost per unit of outcome change is anticipated.

Expert Analysis by Merv Adrian

Research VP, Data & Analytics, Gartner

Like so many stories in healthcare, this one is rich with promise. Combining hitherto separate variables from relatively underutilized data can dramatically improve the efficacy of predictive analytics: more data can deliver richer insights and greater clarity. But there are warning signs: combining sophisticated statistical analysis (often the case with SPSS) with interpretations of interviews, which can be maddeningly different in language across multiple patients and interviewers, is not a task for the faint of heart—or the unskilled.

In understanding such discussions, it's key to dig into details. When is the "anticipated" 42% improvement in outcomes expected? And how will they be measured—and compared to what? What skills will eb required, and does your team have them? If you seek to emulate the methods, be sure that you understand and can reproduce them—and be skeptical about results until you can reproduce them. After all, "data science" is still science—and that is its essence.

46: Screening Customer Data for Root Cause Analysis

#india #asia #content #media #entertainment #television #broadcasting
#movie #music #ecommerce #customer #reporting #monitoring

Zee Entertainment Enterprises is an India-based media and entertainment conglomerate that started in television broadcasts but has now diversified into providing content and media. It has a presence across television broadcasting, movies, music, live entertainment, and digital businesses. It boasts 1.3 billion viewers and 46 domestic channels and 39 international channels in 173 countries. It houses the world's largest Hindi film library and has rights to more than 4,800 movie titles across various languages.

Zee Entertainment ventured into the over-the-top (OTT) TV platform, a streaming service with a globally distributed architecture, with DittoTV in India. It is the country's first over-the-top streaming application by an Indian broadcaster.

With OTT being a new technology, DittoTV found it challenging to consolidate data to generate insights that would bring measurable business value. At that time, the company was using many different data sources like Content Delivery Networks (CDN) logs, life TV schedules, subscriber data, custom applications, and third-party payment gateways. The company wanted to bring together these disparate touchpoints into a streamlined singular platform for improved operational intelligence. It wanted to analyze details such as the content being viewed, its duration, OS, and location, with an aim at increasing its viewership and cutting costs.

From the various sources of data, Zee designed business KPI and operational insights dashboards in real-time, which provided visibility to Ditto TV's product and business teams. The dashboards enabled the viewing of viewer information that included real-time interaction history, device information, a record of errors encountered, etc. The application ecosystem became a valuable tool for the IT Operations Analytics team. It enabled the company to track operation performance, monitor issues, respond to piracy breaches immediately, and prevent streaming and payment failures.

The real-time CRM brought savings of $40,000 in hardware alone. It reduced the root cause analysis time to minutes from days previously. More importantly, it increased the conversion from cold calls by 15% and from support services by 45%.

Expert Analysis by Steve Palmer

President, FactFusion, and retired global
analytics executive with Avanade

Zee Entertainment has taken a strong first step by building a solid, quantifiable data foundation for understanding operational performance of the business. But it is just the beginning. Now with a foundation in place there are a multitude of additional use cases made possible by both the assemblage of data, "the platform," and the exercise of extracting measurable value from data, "the process."

Having successfully completed the beginning of the journey is incredibly valuable and sets the stage for the process of identifying a potential use case or value propositions, expanding and exploiting the platform and discovering value then activating the realization of the value in the business ... where it matters most! It is the constant pursuit of potential value through use cases combined with speed enabled by the platform and the process that will move business forward and allow Zee to respond quickly to evolving markets and customer demands.

47: On Track with Covid Contact Tracing

#china #asia #trains #rail #locomotive #transportation
#travel #dataprocessing #monitoring #alerting #consumer
#covid19 #pandemic #railway #health #safety

The high density of passengers makes the railway the most widely used mass transportation mode in China. A state-owned company, China State Railway Group Company, Limited handles almost all rail operations. The rail transport company was created in 2013 after the dissolution of the Ministry of Railways. Its trains consist of double track, electrified, and high-speed covering a total of 127,000 km (70,000 mi). It has a ridership of 2.36 billion passenger trips and takes 3.81 billion tons freight. The railway has 5,470 stations and stretches across plains, elevations, tunnels, and bridges.

The country's official online railway ticket-booking platform is known as The 12306, which has been generating the railway passenger data of China over the past twenty years. The system has a daily data processing capacity in the hundreds of TB level, and the peak daily number of hits amounts to a trillion level.

Despite cutting trips amid the COVID-19 epidemic, China's railway system managed to carry 12.45 million passenger trips around the mainland as it applies epidemic prevention and control works of the massive flow of train passengers.

After the outbreak of COVID-19, railway authorities launched the emergency response system of its online railway ticket-booking platform 12306. The 12306 system operating team extended the big data analysis and system monitoring to ensure the system's effective operation in coping with the controls in connection with the epidemic.

The big data system proves its advantages particularly with the individual identification and real name ticketing, which are crucial information in tracking the close contacts of travelers diagnosed with the virus. Passengers' real names and mobile photo numbers are registered on the 12306 system. That makes it easy for the railway authorities to cooperate with local governments and epidemic prevention institutions to find the passengers who had close contacts with the COVID-19-diagnosed patients. Making use of the big data, the 12306 system has also started ticketing separate seats to reduce the transmission risk among the riding public.

The China railway group also monitors passengers with fever and as of Feb. 10, 2020, they have found 7,573 passengers with the symptom. They have also assisted in tracking 1,800 batches of passengers who had close contact with diagnosed or suspected of COVID-19.

Expert Analysis by Ian Picache

Data Science Leader, Partner, West Monroe

What strikes me about this article is the conflict between personally identifiable information (PII) vs. the objectives of the greater good. Understanding that China operates under different privacy standards, it is interesting to see the extent China uses private information. In this example, not only do they know names and phone numbers, but they also know where these passengers are and where they traveled from.

Big data projects often have these PII challenges as, by definition, they collect significant amounts of data to generate insights from the actions of many individuals or entities. In most commercial situations, privacy protection is paramount and governs the uses of the data of individuals and customers. Therefore, security measures to protect the data is extremely important.

To take the 12306 system to the next level, it would require real-time integration with other government and epidemic response systems. This way, the government can take rapid action to prevent the spread of COVID-19.

48: Higher Learning Institution Uses Deep Learning to Improve Graduation Rates

#usa #northamerica #university #college #education #academia
#predictive #analytics #modeling #recommendation #customer #student

Georgia State University (GSU) is a large public university in Atlanta with more than 24,000 undergrads. Chartered by the State of Georgia in 1785, the university describes its institution as the birthplace of public higher education in America. The university has a comprehensive reach; its 17 colleges and schools enroll more than 37,000 students and have produced over 315,000 alumni living worldwide. It has campuses in five Georgia locations and Washington D.C. in the US, and England and Italy, as well as partnerships in more than 50 countries on six continents.

GSU is one of the nation's top universities for technology commercialization; it is ranked No. 1 for total products reaching the market, with more than 775 products to date coming from university research. The university is also home to the Peabody Awards, considered the most prestigious prize in electronic media.

Like many public universities, there were limited resources for student advising in GSU. The university has staggering caseloads, a common tendency for large institutions to have. Its student to adviser ratio was 700 a few years ago.

Aware of the benefits predictive analytics brings to consumer businesses, Georgia State University was wondering whether it can apply predictive modeling to an academic environment. It wanted to determine if it could make better use of advisers' time and enable more students to graduate on time.

GSU's analyzed 2.5 million grades earned by students in courses over 10 years. It identified the factors that hurt students' chances for graduation. From the list of the factors, it then applied predictive analytics and built Graduation and Progression Success (GPS), an early-warning system. The system is updated daily. It includes over 700 red flags that will help advisers keep students on track to graduation.

The results from the system prompted 51,000 in-person meetings between advisers and students in the past 12 months. These meetings are mostly adviser-initiated unlike before when they were largely up to the students. In those meetings, advisers discuss actions that the students can do to address issues that may hamper their chances for graduation. The meetings proved effective as graduation rates went up 6%. Additionally, graduates are getting their degrees half a semester sooner compared in the past, which translates to an estimated savings of $12 million in tuition.

Expert Analysis by Shree Bharadwaj

Private Equity and Venture Capital Advisory,
Technology-M&A, West Monroe

This is a great use case on data driven thinking/culture/aware-ness (team fully aware of benefits relating to predictive analytics) that enhanced customer experience (51k collaborations/meetings between advisers and students in the past 12 months) and drove busi-ness outcomes(Savings of $12Mil, with 6% higher graduation points since 2013 and an additional time savings of half a semester). The same approach/model can be utilized by other educational institu-tions to enhance student learning and deliver on better outcomes by leveraging big data and data science (data monetization).

Educational institutions have a rich historical dataset on stu-dents, alumni, faculty, research, location, modalities and outcomes. Leveraging data to automate and provide timely insights for students and faculty that drives adaptive learning and outcomes is critical in this fast-changing world. Considering data fluency across the uni-versity/organization might be varied and siloed, bringing in experts/ consultants (as was the case for Georgia State University) might be a good way to jumpstart on predictive and prescriptive journey while delivering on roadmap initiatives.

What likely challenges for these kinds of projects you have seen that this company likely overcame? or any related opportunities in that industry?

your recommendations for these kinds of initiatives—including what you would recommend taking this kind of solution "to the next level " E.g., how else would they monetize the data, expand on the scope and/or implement this kind of solution in other areas of the business?

Considering Georgia State University was successful in imple-menting the initial predictive use case, improved data fluency across the university would help drive adoption of the solution as well as additional use cases. Additionally, continue to build out predictive models throughout university to further enrich student experience and increase graduation rates will help strengthen its brand.

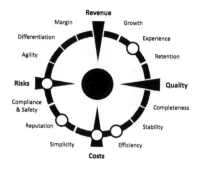

49: VALIDATING VENDOR VERACITY

#usa #northamerica #healthcare #hospital #medical
#wellness #analytics #fraud #alerting #transaction

Memorial Healthcare Systems is one of the largest public health-care systems in the United States. It provides more than 1,900 licensed beds in six hospitals at multiple locations throughout the South Broward County area in Florida. Since its inception in 1953, it has been a leader in providing high-quality healthcare services to South Florida residents. The healthcare system operates several hospitals in Florida, with Memorial Regional Hospital being its flagship facility. Memorial Regional Hospital offers diverse health services in its cardiac and vascular, cancer, and neuroscience institutes.

Highly regarded for its exceptional patient—and family-centered care, Memorial Healthcare Systems has earned prestigious awards. Among them is the honor given by the American Hospital Association, the "Living the Vision" award and the "Foster G. McGaw" award for which Memorial Healthcare was selected from more than 5,000 hospitals as the national model for improving the health of the community.

Memorial Healthcare Systems' hospital network needed transparency in the vendor verification process to prevent frauds from happening and a more efficient invoice processing to improve administrative and overall costs.

Memorial Healthcare deals with vendors that provide products and services such as lab testing and related capital equipment, specialized nursing care, facilities management, construction, and janitorial work.

The healthcare system selected IBM's Big Data analytics and Smarter Content management capabilities to help them with their objectives. IBM, deploying its IBM i2 Intelligence Analysis Platform, and business partner Information Management Consultants (IMC) developed a new vendor vetting system, known as VETTED.

The vendor vetting system collects information from the Memorial Healthcare content management system and cross-references it against 800 internal and external databases. It then analyzes the resulting data to provide insights into the vendor's activities, which were previously not available. In one interesting case, the analytics revealed that three vendors were colluding to price rig a proposal.

Memorial Healthcare now has a fraud management platform across the entire hospital network that reduces risks. Its content management simultaneously speeds up invoice processing. Vendor invoice cycles have been reduced from one month to 18 days on average, which is around 40% time reduction. $2 million ROI will have been achieved over 10 years. The successful Big Data project contributed to a $70 million cost reduction throughout the healthcare system.

Expert Analysis by Bradley Ptasienski

Partner, Data Engineering and Analytics, West Monroe

The data driven fraud solution was a great, innovative way to solve the vendor validation issue that existed at Memorial. The ability to centralize data and insights in the content management system yielded "additional" results in improvements in speed to invoicing and less manual effort. Vendor validation and engagement is obviously not healthcare specific. The notion of data centralization, cleansing, and using AI to make decisions is becoming much more common in the industry. This exact same approach could be utilized in healthcare for provider credentialing, in retail/consumer for upsell or cross sell opportunities, etc. One of the biggest "wins" for this case study was that the AI insights were operationalized and adopted by the health system. Creating an approach that is usable and practical is the key to extracting the most value out of a data driven approach.

Typically, there is a master data challenge that exists with projects like this. Because many of these vendors were likely small, relying on organizations like Dun and Bradstreet to cleanse and enhance data likely yielded spotty results. I'd anticipate that some data cleansing, mapping, and potentially some machine learning enabled matching algorithms were required to make this work successful. Lastly, making the process to utilize the alerts and AI insights usable is incredibly important and typically takes a lot of engagement and effort to get right. Based on positive results being realized outside of the core use case, the organization was able to successfully adopt and action these insights to become a more data-driven organization.

There are a few opportunities for Memorial to consider moving forward: Can the data store that they've created be monetized more broadly in Florida? Can they obtain and aggregate additional data within the state, and offer this service to other health systems or plans as a service? Can the impact on invoices be analyzed further to determine if this is something that can be monetized as well? Perhaps a SAAS approach is viable to extend *invoicing services for other systems? In the same way that Vendor data was aggregated, a very similar approach could be utilized to also streamline Provider credentialization, which could likely drive additional savings.*

50: Directing Ads to the Right People at the Right Time

#usa #northamerica #television #media #entertainment #advertising #marketing #customer #prescriptive #recommendation #monitoring

For *TV advertisers*, the last thing they want is for TV viewers to skip through the commercials of their products or services. To address this concern, DirecTV came up with a way to display ads based on the interest of each household. This way, skipping through commercials or changing channels during program breaks are minimized.

A subsidiary of AT&T, DirecTV is an American satellite-TV subscription service provider headquartered in El Segundo, California, now owned by AT&T. Launched in 1994, DirecTV transmits digital satellite television and audio to its household customers across the United States, Latin America, and the Caribbean servicing about 15 million subscribers.

Robert Gage, Senior Director of Business Intelligence in DirecTV, says, "People generally don't like advertising — but at least if it's something applicable to them, they like it a little bit more." This is the reason why DirecTV started collecting and analyzing its customers' information from internal and external sources and delivering addressable ads to its subscribers. As for advertisers, this plan was also a good idea, because they are now targeting viewers who are more inclined to take action towards their products or services.

DirecTV started this project by gathering and combining proprietary data of its subscribers, including their contact information, program preferences, subscription history, and demographic data from Experian. The company also considered secondary data such as the number of children in the household and the type of car the family uses.

DirecTV analyzes all these available data to help advertisers reach their target audience. When a particular ad is ready to air, data is sent downstream to engineering systems that queue and place targeted ads on specific customers' set-top boxes. Simultaneously, this data is also sent to DirecTV's video measurement vendor so they can track and analyze the number of homes viewing the particular ad.

In its first year of launching, the addressable ads project of DirecTV exceeded its revenue goal by 50%. At present, the project continues to grow exponentially. "It has definitely helped advertisers think differently about purchasing television ads," says James Min, Business Intelligence Solutions Analyst of DirecTV.

Expert Analysis by Ari Kaplan

Global AI Evangelist, Data Robot

For three-quarters of a century, unidirectional televisions and the networks have been feeding us commercials for the average family and generic consumer. In an age where even targeted internet banner ads have been around for a couple decades, it's high time that the cable companies and streaming services have incorporated some smarts into their promotional processes. In fact, whatever business you're in, you should be personalizing your products and services based on who is actually consuming them, in what format, on what device, and at what time.

As Mr. Gage intones in this piece, nobody likes to be average, they want to be special... especially if you want them to engage with you. This is the same in personal relationships as it is in the consumer and business worlds. But even DirecTV didn't have all the data it needed to personalize the experience. Like so many other businesses, they turned to external data sources, integrating them with their own to better understand each viewer. A good lesson here is that if you're a business only staring at the data within your own four walls, you'll never break out of them. Your analytics and intelligence you glean from them will be sorely limited.

And even the analytics part isn't so straightforward. With all that data, it is key to identify how to combine and apply it to determine and affect desired engagement (i.e. consumer behavior) via integrated feedback loops. This kind of intelligence undoubtedly requires just that: artificial intelligence to predict and prescribe behaviors while learning over time.

Going forward, I would expect DirectTV to incorporate additional data sources to KYC (know your customer) even better, develop and incorporate more advanced AI methods, and perhaps find a way to monetize this information externally, not just use it internally.

51: ADVANCING AD EFFICIENCY AND PERFORMANCE

#usa #northamerica #analytics #monitoring #advertising
#seo #marketing #customer #customer

EP+Co is an innovative advertising agency that specializes in shooting and production, video editing, full set design, wood-working, live social videos, and campaign activations. With offices in New York and Greenville, the agency owns a 10,000-foot production and prototyping facility that enables them to create high-quality, production-grade content that is viewable on every screen.

Intending to deliver maximum success for each of their clients, EP+Co draws from 8 disciplines to create successful, integrated user experiences, which include advertising, strategy and planning, production, social content, analytics and research, media, creative technology, and experiential.

One of their notable clients was Advance America, a payday cash loan provider. Through the help of EP+Co, Advance America wanted to grow their business without increasing their marketing budget. They wanted to attract as many leads as possible while reducing effective cost per conversion (eCPC). Since it was difficult to do this using the existing budget, the agency realized that they had to work on placing better measurement and analytics approaches.

To monitor the search and display ads of Advance America, the agency was using the last-touch ad server. However, tracking only users' last touch attribution is not always accurate because it leaves the rest of the customer journey unmeasured. This approach limited the measurement of all touchpoints, channels, and sources.

To move away from last-touch only measurement and get a more holistic view, EP+Co turned to Google Attribution 360, part of the Google Analytics 360 Suite. As a result, EP+Co was able to optimize Advance America's search and display ad campaigns by monitoring the ads' placements, page location, and user-level visibility; and adjusting the budget to placements that yield the best conversions. Furthermore, the tool helped identify non-performing websites and implement frequency caps that prevented wasted expenditures and overlaps of user segments

As a result, EP+Co was able to lower Advance America's campaign effective cost per action (eCPA) by 14 to 20% in the first three months of using Google Attribution 360. It also helped the agency achieve a 19% increase in conversions with the same budget and reduce the overall cost per conversion by 27%. Using Google's advanced analytics suite, the agency got a holistic view of cross-channel marketing performance which enabled them to drive real success for their client.

Expert Analysis by Richard Kessler

Founder and Chief Executive Officer at Classifi

This story highlights the importance of the entire customer journey, the data created along the way, and its relationship to conversion

rates and budgets, as well as the role analytics play in improving conversion rates. Last touch attribution analytics apparently do not capture the complete journey, and instead are focused on an incomplete set of data, potentially leading to false or misleading "insights." Real insights, to improve effective Cost Per Conversion (eCPC) for example, require a highly instrumented "data" journey—with lots of measurements at critical points along the journey—that parallel the customer journey leading up to conversion. An open question is whether or not EP+Co looked at their internal data as well; critics of Google Analytics tools often question whether additional value can be gleaned from looking at both internal and external data, individually and juxtaposed, and not just Cost Per Conversion.

Organizations should examine whether their approaches to analytics are limited, hobbled or even invalidated but misusing analytical tools, using the wrong or incomplete metrics, or insufficiently scoping the data they're accessing. For example, directing analytics towards point-in-time or point-source data sources is limiting. Other approaches can be flawed if they are directed towards internal or external data, but not both. Additionally, if the data is examined through too few "lenses" (i.e., viewpoints of personas), having a single viewpoint into data could obfuscate the true nature of how to improve. Therefore, organizations should take heed of all available data connected with a particular process, product or metric, and examine these many data points from many perspectives to achieve a holistic view and resulting reliable insights.

Often it takes a fresh look at a problem to understand it well enough to ask a different set of questions, and to uncover a flawed approach. There is a benefit to bringing in an outside expert with an unbiased 'fresh set of eyes' to see the data 'elephants' in the room. By understanding budget is impacted throughout the customer journey, EP+Co also understood it needed a different approach to finding all the possible money leaks (e.g., wasted resources) and opportunities (e.g., capabilities that were working) as well as potential new insights (e.g., additional measurements earlier in the journey) to tackle the challenge holistically, and not from one particular perspective.

When organizations take such a holistic approach to data analytics, they may realize the steps taken to get to these improvements (e.g., to get to better outcomes) are indeed also valuable, i.e., valuable and reusable data. These valuable insights can be converted into sets of reusable components (e.g., as part of a microservices architectural approach) that can systematically and repeatably address the same obstacles at other firms, helping them realize the same new efficiencies, and also help them unveil the required telemetry that produces the most value in accelerating their business growth at a fixed or even reduced cost. Although this case focused on a particular metric (eCPC), it doesn't necessarily tell the whole story. Many more metrics are typically required to paint a better and more accurate picture of business growth, leading to better and more predictable outcomes. Such predictions—and the new capabilities that help organizations reach them—can be then monetized into one or more products. For example, the data can be either be repurposed and sold directly (after de-risking) or converted into a money-making service (e.g., eCPC optimizer). New and updated analytics approaches can therefore be made reusable and therefore lead to new products, which can have incredible value compared to the original benefit they products, when used repeatedly to produce better, more predictable business growth at other organizations.

52: No More Phoning-In Teen Telco Services

#newzealand #asiapacific #telecommunications #broadband
#television #network #datastrategy #cloud #customer #predictive

Vodafone New Zealand is a telecommunications company operating in New Zealand. A subsidiary of the London-listed company with the same name, Vodafone offers world-class mobile, broadband, and landline services, as well as a TV network.

While the company is among the top telco providers in the country, one of its biggest challenges is their ability to provide relevant offers to prepay customers. "This prevents Vodafone New Zealand from capitalizing on opportunities to upsell and cross-sell services and products. Customers were also potentially missing out on deals and offers that would improve their experience," David Bloch, manager for analytics and data strategy of Vodafone NZ, shares.

Because prepay customers are not required to submit any personal information when buying SIM cards, Vodafone did not have any demographics data that they can use to reach out and market to this customer segment. To address this, Vodafone NZ sought the help and service of Teradata, the world's leading provider of pervasive data intelligence, data and analytics solutions, and hybrid cloud products. By partnering with Teradata, Vodafone NZ was able to utilize big data in accurately predicting the traits and behaviors of their prepay customers.

In the absence of real customer data, Vodafone NZ worked with Teradata to identify patterns and behaviors of most of their user base, which they will eventually apply across their entire customer database. To do this, they took advantage of the Teradata Aster appliance, an analytics tool that leverages the open-source Hadoop big data ecosystem, and R analytics software, helping them determine possible demographic segment groups.

Within just four weeks of using the systems, Teradata was able to capture 2.6 million connections that generated data usage traffic on the network, 38.4 billion individual application sessions by users, and 85.4 million different IP addresses accessed by users.

With all these data in hand, including predictive user patterns, Vodafone was able to understand its key customer segment behavior, which helped them create and implement well-targeted campaigns that deliver better results.

As a result, the new solution has enabled Vodafone NZ to achieve an 89% correct prediction ratio. They were able to determine a huge amount of youth customers in its user base. Hence, the company decided to transition into a new youth proposition called Vodafone Mates.

Expert Analysis by Wayne Eckerson

President, Eckerson Group

What's interesting about this case is that Vodafone NZ was still able to understand its customers and their behavior even in the absence of customer data. In other words, Vodafone NZ was able to piece together aggregate customer profiles and demographics from usage data alone—that is, by phone calls rather than the phone callers. We don't know all the magic that went into the analysis—what algorithms were used and models created. That's not insignificant capital, but it sounds like Vodafone NZ's data provider helped kick-start the effort with some of its own models and data scientists.

By definition, usage data is voluminous, and it's the future of data analytics. Very few companies today—even many high-tech companies—know how to exploit this untapped resource. Understanding how customers use products reveals a host of insights that can help product development, engineering, security (fraud), and, of course, sales and marketing. In the near future, information about how customers use products will be more valuable than the products themselves. And, in some industries, this data can be monetized, adding another source of revenue for the company.

53: Revving-Up Manufacturing Efficiency

#usa #northamerica #transportation #vehicle
#manufacturing #safety #telemetry

Harley-Davidson, Inc. is an American-based manufacturer and marketer of heavyweight motorcycles and related products. With a market cap of $6B, manufacturing operations across the United States, Brazil, India and Thailand, and annual production of 200,000 motorcycles, the company is one of the largest motorcycle manufacturers in the world with an industry reputation for manufacturing quality and performance.

With an already lean workforce in a constrained labor market, leadership at Harley's 850,000 sqft drivetrain manufacturing facility in Menomonee Falls, Wisconsin faced unique constraints in addressing the company's call for belt tightening and incremental safety. The team recognized their need for technology-driven efficiency gains, but still felt the sting of previous investments in solutions that promised savings from machine monitoring and fell short because they could not translate Harley's existing operational data into meaningful bottom-line results. Instead, those providers called upon Harley to double-down on their investments with sweeping telemetry upgrades to improve data quality and availability, and thereby enable the solutions—a pill that was too hard to swallow, even in the pre-pandemic environment.

Nearly convinced that major investment in data-creation was required to unlock meaningful margin improvements, leadership at the drivetrain facility engaged to identify, pilot, and comparatively evaluate solutions that claimed the ability to improve production efficiency and reliability. Ultimately, Harley selected Golgix, a manufacturing-focused lean AI provider offering a unique solution to the data quality and availability challenge. Instead of recommending more hardware deployment or upgrades for data generation, Golgix's platform creates a large volume of structured derived data from few available unstructured machine data points and uses that derived data to train contextually predictive models for efficiency improvements and machine failures.

Plant leadership decided to pilot the technology on a subset of their aluminum milling computer numerical control (CNC) machines. Even with strong baseline performance and adherence to industry best practices, CNC machine extended cycle times and unplanned downtime were restraining production capacity and driving variation to production plans. With only 28 days of raw operating data from the CNC machines' on-board controllers, the technology predicted 91% of machine failures. This enabled Harley to increase production capacity by 8–10% by reducing unplanned downtime. Altogether, the technology enabled plant personnel and leadership to visualize real-time machine and cell level Lean KPIs, quantify production losses, and respond proactively to real-time machine and tool failure predictions with root cause analyses.

In creating a more predictable production environment with greater visibility into overall equipment effectiveness (OEE), availability, performance, quality and first pass yield (FPY), leadership also gained the ability to engage in production planning with added insight and simplicity. Furthermore, with increased production capacity, the solution provides the flexibility to ramp up faster in the wake of COVID, minimizing production-driven constraints on revenue generation as supply chains, distribution and demand normalized.

54: Social Services Organization Fraught with Fraud No More

#australia #asiapacific #disability #disasterrecovery #youthjustice #domesticviolence #health #safety #frauddetection #automation #datalake #socialservices #humanservices #welfare

The Department of Human Services (DHS) is an Executive Agency of the Australian Government that delivers a range of services, funding, and policy responsibilities, which support fairness, opportunity, and choice for Australians. On behalf of the Australian government, it leads the responsibility in the areas of disability, disaster recovery, youth justice, domestic violence, screening services, and early intervention to support health, safety, and wellbeing of children. Its services include welfare, health, and child support payments, etc. to eligible Australian citizens and permanent residents. The department provides various grants to community organizations and concessions. It also leads policy responsibility concerning women, youth, and volunteers.

The Department of Human Services aims to return $1.7 billion to government coffers that were lost from welfare fraud and debts. It used to rely on manual data-matching processes to detect anomalies, which were not only costly but ineffective.

The DHS corroborated with AUSTRAC, the anti-money laundering agency, in a four-year data matching project to improve the government's ability to detect persons who receive welfare benefits with unexplained wealth. AUSTRAC received $21.1 million to build the analytic platform for the DHS-led project.

The agency developed an automated data-matching process that uses an open-source architecture platform based on Greenplum database and Apache Spark processing engine. Along with Talend integration software, they are the components of a broader data lake.

Using the data analytics platform, the DHS has initially recovered over $25 million in fraudulent welfare payments from over 650 welfare recipients reviews in just its first year of implementation. The new platform's other current application is its use in large-scale statistical risk modeling in money laundering and counterterrorism.

Expert Analysis by Marty Ellingsworth

Senior Analyst, Celent

They struck pay-dirt here. I love these types of "found money" problems, but I hate that they persist. When it comes to cheating people out of their money, especially by fraud, waste, and abuse of government programs, it is the most embarrassing part of my professional life to see successful projects.

Especially projects where the key attributes are: 1) access to data long locked away from analytics; 2) basic data hygiene is used to clean up payee identity; 3) reviewing resolved payee records finds multiple payments, overpayments, and mis-payments; 4) basis data matching to other control databases alerts even more mis-payments;

and, 5) success metrics include "stopping stupid payments" along with recovery of past improper payments.

It is professionally sad that these successes date back earlier than the 1980's, yet the basics of controlling payments to poorly identified payees propagates still today in most organizations.

We should all invest more in identity graphs and pre-payment data quality and cross database validation work.

55: CASHING-IN WITH ADVANCED ANALYTICS

#croatia #europe #banking #financial #investment
#asset #modeling #predictive #analytics #transformation
#datamining #document #customer

Zagrebačka banka d.d. or Zagrebačka Bank (ZABA) is the biggest bank in Croatia. Based in Zagreb and one of the country's biggest employers, it is one of the most profitable subsidiaries of the Italian Unicredit Group. Its services include private banking, investment banking, corporate banking, and asset management. With 130 branches and 850 ATMs, the bank serves 1.1 million private customers out of Croatia's 4.1 million citizens. It also has 80,000 corporate clients. ZABA contributes greatly to the Croatian economy. It controls 35% of the country's investment funds, 41% of obligatory pension funds, and 30% of specialized savings accounts for real estate transactions. The bank accounts for 25% of Croatia's banking sector's total assets and almost 60% of its profits.

ZABA saw the need to improve statistical modeling and predictive analytics, which used to take three days for data preparation and model scoring and at least 24 hours for model building. The process involved moving large volumes of financial and customer data between servers and databases to generate predictive analytics. It entailed several dedicated hardware resources, specialized manpower, and the cost and risks that go with the setup. It made the ability to use predictive analytics for commercial activities in order to better target customers for new banking products and services difficult.

ZABA switched to Oracle Advanced Analytics on Oracle Database to transform its traditional predictive analytics process into a seamless process that performs all tasks, including data import and export, data transformation, model building, and model scoring. They are all executed within the database in seconds, minutes, or hours—in a fraction of time compared to the old process. Moving data and dedicated analytical servers are no longer necessary as analyzing is done on Oracle Database. Computations on thousands of attributes are executed with Oracle Advanced Analytics, which is impossible with open-source R. Analysts are able to leverage in-database mining algorithms with both Oracle Advanced Analytics' Oracle Data Mining and Oracle' R enterprise components for much faster access to analytics data such as credit risk scoring and customer retention.

The use of the Oracle platform increased ZABA's agility, enabling it to make quality decisions on time, increasing its cash loan business 15% within 18 months due to improved hit ratio. Through a more rapid delivery of predictive analytics from the Oracle system, decision making across the bank's commercial and regulatory activities was strengthened. It enables risk managers to improve credit risk scoring with a fast ad-hoc analysis. The need for dedicated analytical servers with specialized manpower was eliminated, improving the total cost of ownership.

Expert Analysis by Anita Toth

Chief Churn Crusher at anitatoth.ca

There is often a reluctance in large companies to replace traditional data systems or processes, despite being outdated and requiring significant manual effort. Investing into a new data system, like ZABA did with Oracle Advanced Analytics, can be daunting and fraught with challenges. The implementation process requires a well-planned rollout that minimally impacts both employees and customers.

Encouraging adoption of the new system can have dramatic results, as seen in the ZABA story. Speed to data, allowing for quality and quick decision-making not only bettered company outcomes but also impacted the level of service ZABA employees were able to provide to customers. Simply put, access to better and faster data leads to improved customer and company outcomes.

Going forward, ZABA should continue to look for other legacy systems and processes that, when replaced, can have a similar, powerful impact on the desired outcomes of both the company and customers alike.

56: Finding Financial Aid Fraud Faster

#usa #northamerica #education #academia #college
#university #predictive #analytics #reporting #storage
#datawarehouse #student #customer #financial

Ivy Tech Community College of Indiana is the largest post-secondary educational institution and singly accredited statewide community college system in the United States, offering more than 150 programs, more than 100 transfer programs, and more than 1,000 online classes. The public community college was established in 1963 as Indiana's Vocational Technical College, offering technical and vocational education to support various industries. In 1999, it was rechartered as a system of community colleges, and renamed Ivy Tech Community College of Indiana. It has close to 200,000 enrolled students and 9,000 faculty across 23 campuses in 560 locations in the US.

Ivy Tech's data infrastructure requirements are enormous. It has 24,000 school-owned PCs, 1,200 applications, and 2,000 wireless access points. It deals with 23 million email transmissions daily as well as 10 terabytes of information downloaded from the internet daily. The large student population in the community college leads to an ongoing database with about 1.7 million records. Ivy Tech needed an operational data store (ODS) to mine petabytes of student data. It also must solve the query wait times of 40 minutes, which was paralyzing the system.

Ivy Tech employed the services of Amazon Web Services (AWS). The school's raw data was stored in Amazon's S3 buckets before uploading into the Amazon Redshift, to perform predictive analytics and produce reports using software from Pentaho, an AWS technology partner and Wolfram Mathematica. The predictive analytics performed with the new system yielded more than 70% accuracy.

Ivy Tech Community College now can effectively store and analyze petabyte scale data at much lower costs than other enterprise data warehouse solutions. And they can actively monitor student performance early in the semester to quickly identify and counsel those at risk of failing. With queries take as little as three seconds, down from 40 minutes or more before, the college can detect issues like financial aid fraud that might have taken days to discern in the past.

Expert Analysis by Stephen Diorio

Executive Director of the Revenue Enablement Institute

The most important part of this story is that the university saw need and defined the need to harness and manage their raw student data as a business priority. In doing so, they not only came up with a coherent enterprise data strategy but were able to create value for the students and the university immediately. By reducing the time and cost involved in mining previously unstructured student data, they were able to create value by proactively aiding student success (graduation rate), reducing business risks (like fraud) and lowering overall operating costs. Perhaps equality important, they removed the technical and time barriers to—a big step towards creating a more data driven culture.

Going forward, this company might consider using this data to create more value as they become more sophisticated. Their focus on student success can be refined further by to identify specific learning needs or new learning paths to help students get the most benefit from their academic journey. For example, they can borrow from the business community and put in place readiness and reinforcement programs that mine student interaction and performance data to identify specific learning needs and delivering focused resources (e.g., classes, learning modules, assignments, or tools) to help them address the more specific issues. They can create or tailor curriculum that meets new or previously unidentified needs or learning gaps by taking a 360-degree view of performance.

Two challenges they are likely to face as they evolve this program will be, making sure the view is worth the climb and brining more non-technical stakeholders into the process to ensure. It is smart to understand the fixed and variable costs associated with developing new use cases, and a financially valid scorecard for assessing and prioritizing the right the most profitable opportunities. And as use cases expand, the team will need to bring in non-technical experts with domain expertise needed to structure the learning programs or financial models needed to create value with the data.

57: HIGH-FLYING DATA FUELS DOWN-TO-EARTH ANALYTICS

#australia #asiapacific #energy #utilities #predictive #prescriptive #cloud #reporting #monitoring #video

F ugro Roames was founded as a business unit within Ergon Energy to provide asset management services to clients of the Queensland-based electricity distribution network operator and retailer. It had the unique challenge of managing Australia's most geographically distributed network, which consisted of an AU$11.5 billion asset base distributed over 150,000km of overhead power lines. Its biggest task was to ensure clearance of vegetation away from the overhead lines to minimize the risk of service disruption, fires, and electrocution.

Ergon Energy divested the Roames unit to the Netherlands-based Fugro to offer the same benefits to power companies worldwide. Currently, Fugro Roames operates aircraft equipped with cameras and laser sensors that fly over customers' networks and capture data. The business then runs analytics and sends reports used by teams to prioritize maintenance and preservation activities.

Fugro Roames started operations with an on-premises data center using servers, storage, networking, and associated systems. It was using traditional computing tools in an environment requiring a super-computer capability. They were vulnerable to system maintenance cooling shutdowns. Also, the more capacity they added to cope with demand peak periods, the more cooling they needed and the more prohibitive the costs became. Fugro Roames needed to enhance its physical infrastructure with capabilities for analysis of demand peak periods and to predict future demand.

Amazon Web Services (AWS) was recommended for alternative infrastructure options for Fugro Roames' data capture, analysis, and reporting systems. The migration to the cloud was initiated, and all workloads run in an AWS infrastructure today.

Raw data from numerous sources is loaded into a server and sent over a 10GB per second AWS Direct Connect link to an AWS architecture running in Amazon VPC, a virtual private cloud. Raw and interpreted data is stored in Amazon S3, while resizable compute power is provided by Amazon EC2, a combination of on-demand and reserved instances running in Windows or Linux operating systems.

Adept use of Amazon EC2 Spot Instances—unused EC2 capacity available in the AWS cloud offered at up-to 90% off of On-Demand prices—has helped Fugro Roames reduce the cost of heavy computing work. A database running in Amazon DynamoDB supports concurrent access from a cluster of Amazon EC2 Spot Instances, while the interpreted data is sent to Amazon Glacier for archiving. Messages are distributed between various components of the AWS architecture using Amazon SQS. An Amazon Redshift data warehouse batches and models information for clients. Amazon CloudFront is used as the content delivery network between the VPC and end-users, while Elastic Load Balancing is used to attenuate traffic.

This implementation has enabled Ergon Energy to reduce the annual cost of vegetation management from AU$100 million to AU$60 million, and technology capital costs have fallen by 95%. Moreover, the business no longer requires a team of five employees dedicated to infrastructure management.

Expert Analysis by Kevin McIsaac

Manager, Data and Analytics, Deloitte Australia

Fugro Roames have created a fantastic solution that was born out real world business needs. A common feature of highly successful analytics projects is an early and strong focus on the business outcome. On the other hand, IT centric projects, often focused on capturing, storing and cleaning data, or experimenting with a technology or platform, are much typically less successful.

A too often overlooked critical success factor for "AI projects" is the clear identification of the business value, in this case an "annual reduction in the cost of vegetation management" by 40 million AUD. WIth such large, and easily explained benefit the project team would have easily justified the investments. Data driven projects often require significant and costly computing resources, which need to be justified by the business value. As in this case, the scale of computing required, which can vary significantly hour by hour, is usually better accommodated by a hyperscale cloud than an on-premises infrastructure.

58: WEB CONTENT HARVESTING HELPS CITIZENS FIND A SHOT

#covid #vaccine #vaccination #webdata #webcontent #webcrawling #healthcare #medicine #pharma #dataforgood

FindAShot.org is an automated COVID-19 vaccine appointment checker system. It was born out of the challenges the founder, David Newell encountered when helping his parents try to find a COVID-19 vaccine appointment. With access to public data, Newell has enabled all Americans access to, and the ability to book COVID-19 vaccinations with ease and simplicity.

After doing some research into the COVID-19 vaccine appointments system, Newell understood that every pharmacy was going to have a different website for booking appointments. He understood very quickly that this method would become very painful and inefficient.

That started the process of building an online appointment checker that would check all of the pharmacy websites to see if they, essentially, had vaccine appointment availability. From there, it was about automating this checking process.

After finding appointments for his parents, he realized that other people were going to need help finding appointments over the next several months, and that's when findashot.org was born— a community service project that would help people find available COVID-19 vaccination appointments at local pharmacies. It started with Albertsons brands (e.g., Tom Thumb, Safeway, Vons, Acme), and then expanded to Kroger and, eventually, Walgreens and CVS. Now, the organization covers 20,000–25,000 locations nationwide. Instead of having to frequently search every single individual pharmacy location to find an available appointment, findashot.org is like a "KAYAK" for COVID-19 vaccine appointments—one streamlined search shows all pharmacy locations that currently have appointments available.

Shortly after its launch findashot.org was adding more than 2000 users per week. Moreover, its helping vaccine thousands of distribution centers from having to throw out millions of doses because they expire shortly after being taken out of cold storage.

FindAShot.org uses the Bright Data Web Unlocker, thanks to The Bright Initiative. It has helped the project scale its ability to perform automated online data collection. In most cases, the pharmacies put in place preventative measures to stop "bad actors" from accessing the site. Newell talked about nefarious individuals automatically booking appointments and then selling them. The mechanisms pharmacies have in place also block the good traffic like FindAShot. org's; simply trying to help people find appointments. The Bright Data Web Unlocker has helped them get unblocked in situations where they have encountered some of those issues that block the appointment checkers. It has also helped reduce the costs of their infrastructure because instead of trying to spin up new appointment checkers somewhere else to get unblocked, they simply switched over and used the Unlocker to integrate into the existing checkers.

Expert Analysis by Doug Laney

Innovation Fellow, Data & Analytics Strategy, West Monroe | Professor of Infonomics, University of Illinois Gies College of Business

Is there any better data-for-good example than a rapid startup that harvests content from across the web to help keep millions of people alive and well? Even just a decade ago this kind of solution would be hampered by an inability to efficiently gather all the necessary data in near real-time. Today, with so many websites blocking crawlers and setting up "I'm not a robot" authentication and other validation gauntlets, utilities like those from Bright Data can find a non-nefarious purpose.

Kudos to Mr. Newell for so clearly seeing a problem staring him in the face then conceiving and developing a straightforward solution to it. Large organizations continue to suffer from their own weight when it comes to implementing solutions like this. Even with teams of data scientists and data lakes full of (mostly underleveraged) information, organizational inertia, process, regulations, politics, lack of data literacy, and cultural inhibitors contribute to their sluggishness. This happens in every industry.

Findashot.org should be an inspirational example to business leaders as to the art of the possible—not just with their own data, but by harvesting, integrating, and analyzing freely available data sources. And it should shame them to higher levels of data literacy and agility.

59: Harvesting and Sharing Data to Seed Research

#usa #northamerica #research #patent #consolidated
#recommendation #document #legal #webcontent

The *Federal Laboratory Consortium* for Technology Transfer (FLC) is the formally chartered, nationwide network of over 300 federal laboratories, agencies, and research centers in the United States. It fosters commercialization best practice strategies and opportunities for accelerating federal technologies from out of the labs and into the marketplace.

The organization promotes industry, business, and job creation from new technology developed in the laboratories. It also facilitates technology transfer (T2) to help businesses to succeed. Through its initiatives, FLC ensures that the American taxpayers' investments in the federal laboratories for research and development and scientific and technological breakthrough efforts benefit the people and return dividends to the economy.

The FLC was organized in 1974 and formally chartered by the Federal Technology Transfer Act of 1986. Its host agency is the National Institute of Standards and Technology.

As a leader in maximizing collaborative research and technology transfer among its member laboratories, the FLC is committed to providing high quality services and cutting-edge tools necessary for labs to successfully carry out their mandated T2 missions.

The data that FLC kept like patent information was fragmented and spread across more than 40 technology transfer websites, each with a different structure and information hierarchy. Manually consolidating this fragmented data and keeping it up to date was not a practical option. The FLC business site needed to aggregate data like lab facilities, equipment, funding, patents, etc. across all federal laboratories into one searchable database.

FLC decided it needed to revamp the FLC business website to make it organized, reliable, and user-friendly. With the use of Connotate (now Import.io), patent information is extracted every week from more than 40 individual technology transfer sites. The tool normalizes and stores all information in a consistent schema, creating an up-to-date, searchable patent database.

FLC Business website now delivers accurate patent information from more than 340 distributed federal laboratories and research institutions.

Expert Analysis by John Lucker

Executive Vice President, Chief Strategy & Analytics Officer,
Universal Fire & Casualty Insurance Company

The challenges of database construction for complex text and scientific information can be very challenging. While portions of utility and business method patent applications and issued patents contain reliable structured data with clear meaning attributable to the tags and field contents, much of the prose of patents are written in ways that make parsing and standardization of terminology via AI and text processing methods very challenging.

Often patents are crafted to be deliberately general—and sometimes misleading—while also being specific enough to allow the patent to "own" the IP of the methods and innovations. Embedded terms and concepts are often combined and crafted to cast a wide net to allow the patent to incorporate a broad landscape of ideas even if the patent itself is inherently specific.

As a result, it seems inevitable that the FLC business website doesn't always yield purity of intended results. My expectation is that the best the FLC patent harmonization effort has achieved is a physical consolidation of information among the 340 lab sites with some useful keyword indexing based on structured data fields but to actually find what a user is looking for requires an additional layer of manual labor (reading and research) to whittle down the search results based on the true meaning, context, and content of the patents being reviewed.

In the end, there's likely no getting around the need for individual expertise that is familiar with optimal search methodologies, indexing standards, and general topical expertise that understands what is being searched for and how to interpret the relevance of highly complex search results of esoteric scientific information.

60: Assimilated Patient Data Saves Lives

#usa #northamerica #health #healthcare #medical
#cloudera #datamanagement #datahub #patient
#customer #monitoring #recommendation

Cerner Corporation is an American provider of health information technology solutions services, devices, and hardware. Cerner solutions are contracted at more than 27,500 facilities in over 35 countries.

Cerner's goal is to deliver more than software and solutions by leveraging electronic medical records (EMR) to help improve health and care across the board. It aims to assimilate and normalize the world's healthcare data in order to increase efficiency of delivering healthcare, improving patient outcomes, and reduce cost.

To accomplish this, the firm needed the ability to iterate quickly on search processing algorithms and build a comprehensive view of population health on a Big Data platform by bringing together all the world's health data.

Cerner chose Cloudera enterprise data hub powered by Apache Hadoop for its analytic data management platform. By utilizing

Cloudera's enterprise data hub, the company is expanding beyond its traditional focus on EMR. Aside from ingesting multiple different EMRs, the platform also takes in Health Level 7 (HL7) feeds, Health Information Exchange information, claims data, and custom extracts from a variety of proprietary or client-owned data sources.

The data is then pushed into the appropriate Apache HBase or HDFS cluster using Apache Storm.

Now Cerner's enterprise data hub contains more than two petabytes (PB) of data in a multi-tenant environment, supporting several hundred clients. To-date, Cerner clients have already reported that the new system has helped save hundreds of lives by providing more accurate predictions around patient health.

Expert Analysis by Sandro Saitta

Chief Industry Advisor, Swiss Data Science Center

One of the most time-consuming steps in data science is to bring data from different sources together. When central systems containing all the needed data are in place, the efficiency gain for end users is tremendous. This use case shows that it is feasible to collect and store data from various sources and make it accessible to different stakeholders for further analytics. Breaking data silos is a key step to generate more value from existing data.

Now that the system is in place, one of the main challenges is to keep data definition up to date. This is key to avoid shifting from a data lake to a data swamp. A potential next step would be to allow different stakeholders to share their specific data, on top of the existing data lake, and leverage the power of federated learning. Customers would be able to apply machine learning on a larger set of data sources—while preserving privacy—and save even more lives.

61: CLEVERLY CONFIGURING CREDIT CARD CAMPAIGNS

#china #asia #banking #financial #datawarehouse #mpp
#query #digitaltransformation #customer #document

China CITIC Bank (CCB) is a Hong Kong-based full-service commercial bank that offers a broad spectrum of financial services spanning wealth management, wholesale banking, personal banking, as well as global markets and treasury solutions. It has 28 branches and two business banking centers in Hong Kong, as well as branches and presence in Beijing, Shanghai, Shenzhen, and Macau, and overseas branches in Singapore, New York, and Los Angeles. While maintaining a strong foothold on the mainland banking industry, CCB operates in almost 130 countries.

CCB was running disparate systems and a physical hardware platform designed for supporting single applications, which significantly delayed access to customer data. It also used a tape storage solution to meet regulatory requirements, which made data extraction slow and difficult to scale. It needed to integrate the bank's data systems & platforms to make use of growing customer data and improve competitiveness.

It identified the need for a centralized, highly scalable data warehouse solution that could integrate with the bank's FICO TRIAD Customer Management Solution, Database Marketing platform, IBM Cognos Business Intelligence software and subcenter customer relationship management (CRM) system.

CCB chose Pivotal Greenplum for its centralized enterprise data warehouse solution. A solution built on an open platform, it provided massively parallel processing (MPP) architecture for data loading and parallel query processing. The bank transformed its legacy systems data and used a data warehouse solution to enable multi-user collaboration across 11 departments and analytical systems.

The transformation resulted in a lot of benefits for CCB. Marketing has successfully conducted more than 1,200 marketing campaigns and has reduced its average configuration time for each campaign by 86%. The bank has streamlined its minimum delivery time—reducing it from two weeks to 2–3 days. Credit Card Center has already gained up to 40 times the investment in Pivotal Greenplum. Moreover, the new technology improved business agility making CCB more highly responsive to customer requests and changes in transaction data, which helps significantly reduce risk, while still serving its customers and meeting their credit needs.

Expert Analysis by Robert Smallwood

CEO & Publisher at *IG World Magazine*, Institute for IG, Chairman at Certified IG Officers Association

This is an example of a dramatic success in implementing an information technology solution to address key business needs. However, it does not tell the whole story.

The business results of implementing the new data warehouse platform cannot be entirely attributed to the system implementation itself. To attain these types of outstanding results, CCB must have also had a robust data governance program in place, with a focus on data quality. Because without good, clean, accurate data, gaining significant business results would have been impossible.

Having a solid and mature data governance program in place will help other organizations achieve the types of gains that CCB was able to make when implementing new technologies.

Also, CCB must have had a very talented, thorough, and methodical project management team and approach. They obviously executed on achieving project milestones in a timely fashion and were likely tracking the project's progress with detailed metrics.

Moving forward, now that CCB has gained significant benefits from the new data warehousing solution, they should look for other ways to fully exploit the platform. Perhaps they could roll it out for additional applications and look for opportunities to leverage the new capability using analytics to deliver profound new insights to reduce risk, improve compliance capabilities, or find opportunities to apply principles of infonomics. This may mean looking for external data sources to combine with internally generated data points, and searching for new insights to add value, which could result in finding some new opportunities to actually monetize data. Or the result could be simply providing more and better information to targeted departments to optimize their operational efficiency. In any case, they have a great platform to build upon.

62: Mining Mining Data Improves Production Tons

#usa #northamerica #mining #naturalresources
#ai #modeling #sensors #recommendation

B ased in Phoenix, Arizona, Freeport-McMoRan is the producer of the world's largest publicly traded copper and operates large mines of gold, molybdenum, and copper in geographically diverse locations. The company performs major operations in North and South America, the Grasberg district in Indonesia which has one of the largest copper-gold deposits in the world, and large-scale mineral districts in Arizona. In 2018, the company was looking to devise a $200 million expansion plan to increase capacity at its massive and complex Bagdad copper mine.

Months after this expensive expansion plan began the works, copper prices dropped putting Freeport-McMoRan in a tight situation of needing an immense capital outlay. But instead of doing that, the company built an AI model that wrung out more productivity out of their Bagdad mining site. Data extracted from this model revealed that historical "recipes," which dictated the mining

191

process, were limiting Freeport's potential for getting more out of the Bagdad mine.

The model, analyzing three years of data from thousands of sensors at the mine, led to major changes in their ways of extracting copper. Originally, it was assumed that the ores entering the mill were of the same type but with the model integrating data from sensors all around each project, seven distinct types of ore were identified and revealed that the mill's control standards did not match those properties.

With this discovery, Freeport adopted new techniques to improve ore recovery. The team adjusted controls to accommodate each of the seven types and this enhanced their copper production by over 10%. Making changes in their vast flotation tanks that altered the potential hydrogen (pH) levels also resulted in increased and enhanced copper extraction.

Freeport's Bagdad mine has now boosted its production by 9,000 metric tons. This impressive production increase would have required major capital investments of no less than $1.5 billion to $2 billion. But for Freeport-McMoRan to realize such gains by analytics alone is a major breakthrough in the mining industry.

Expert Analysis by Tom Hulsebosch

Sr. Managing Director, Chicago Office Lead, West Monroe

This cases study shows how more real-time analysis of the input ingredients to the processing of natural resources can be used to make real-time changes to the process to optimize the refined product. This is true when converting from ore to cooper or when taking crude oil and turning it into a variety of oil-based products. Data analytics can be very helpful in showing us the optimal process based on analysis of director and indirect sensory data associated with the ingredients.

AI opportunities are beginning to appear in refining many different natural resources. The proliferation of sensory data from the process and about the raw material contents is making it possible to adapt the refining process based on this sensory information to drive up margins, lower waste, and improve stakeholder returns.

63: Innovative Data Flow Boosts Water Savings and Maintenance

#uk #europe #utilities #conservation #sustainability #iot #ai

#monitoring #prescriptive #machinelearning #customer

Founded to help users save money and improve natural resource management, Conservation Labs is an Amazon Alexa Fund portfolio company with the mission of more cost-effective and sustainable water use. Homelync, a provider of an open platform for IoT integration in UK social landlords, takes space in the social housing industry and shares the same mission as Conservation Labs. With Homelync as its client, Conservation Labs invented a non-invasive smart water technology that is affordable and simply attaches over a pipe which means learning to use it is easy for the regular water consumers.

Almost 20% of housing in the UK is for the most vulnerable in the country. This translates to five million units intended for the use of those who often have the final access to IoT and AI technology. The original approach for supplying water in these properties resulted in tons of wasted water use which was not only costly but also hurting the natural water sources. The initiative was aimed at finding a solution to conserve water by pinpointing crucial areas that contributed to water wastage such as leaks, improper resource management, power consumption, and more.

H2know solves these problems as it can quantify and classify all water use including the detection of leaks in real-time. This approach takes thousands of sound measurements per second from a pipe and converts them to proprietary values through an audible sound range which then converts them into data for usable water insights. It also uses a proprietary machine-learning method that relies on a range of analytic techniques including neural networks. Additionally, the approach accounts for relevant factors that balance timeliness with risk, cost, and power consumption by optimizing edge-to-cloud computations.

The results of the H2know initiative support the common mission of Conservation Labs and Homelync to enable sustainable and more cost-effective water use with consideration of the social good. Analysis showed that H2know has translated to a savings of more than 4 million gallons of water and 1.3mKg of CO_2 for landlords for the first 10,000 properties. This is equivalent to a $500,000 reduction of water and maintenance costs per year for the landlords and their residents.

Expert Analysis by Daniel Belmont

Managing Director, Energy & Utilities Practice Lead, West Monroe

Conservation and sustainability have been in corporate vernacular for a number of years. Only recently through the use of low-cost advanced edge communications technologies can individual user business cases aimed at things like power conservation and water loss make a substantial impact in curbing water loss and CO_2 emissions when rolled out across a market. With the increased push for global decarbonization, mandated CO2 reduction goals will add another positive financial impact to this equation.

Furthermore, this firms and the water industry in particular could look to the insurance industry to assist in offsetting this investment and possibly license their data since leakage leads to damage and is responsible for more than $10B a year in water damage claims in the U.S. alone. This improves the business case even more and is a win-win-win-win for the consumer, HomeLync, insurance companies, and the planet.

This is a monetization of data investment that can be made by the providers with no out of pocket for the most vulnerable consumers that helps them contribute to the greater good and save money.

64: DIGITAL TWIN ELIMINATES NEED FOR MORE PEOPLE

#turkey #europe #insurance #home #health #sla #reporting #customer #document #visualization #digitaltwin

The Turkish insurance company, Aksigorta, aimed to optimize inefficient processes in traditional insurance companies. Initially, they found this initiative to be quite a challenge because of the barriers between conventional ways of doing business and modern advanced approaches. The transition between these two worlds has very rough friction. That is until Aksigorta made a breakthrough as they identified an opportunity to use digital twin technology to enhance and adopt more efficient business processes.

Aksigorta's motive for finding the optimal solution to transitioning the traditional approaches in their insurance company to advanced optimal methods stems from the big challenges that insurers face in this ordeal. Insurers agree on the difficulty of finding real pain points in the business especially when the different departments of the business function in silos instead of a more coherent flow. Moreover, this attempt at change creates friction between insurer companies and their agency partners as well as customers. A bigger challenge is rooted in managing the expectations and behaviors of the customers with the transition.

Through digital twin technology, Aksigorta made digital copies of their business process in Digital Mirror, a virtual platform that improves measurability and provides end-to-end visibility for these processes. Digital Mirror also provides insurers with granular insights from agencies and customers hence solving the big challenge of managing customer behavior and expectation. It enables companies to provide the customer's desired services without comprising SLAs or service-level agreements. With this high-functioning platform, insurers are provided with the intelligence on critical pain points that are not based on traditional measures, like subjective staff evaluations, but on real statistical data.

Thanks to the creation of a digital twin of their business units, Aksigorta can optimize business processes in just months. It also provided clear forecast visualization of end-to-end process cycles, data-based insights useful in better decision-making, better KPI monitoring, and more.

In seven months, the insurer executed these 11 sprints in their operations. Digital Mirror redesigned six main processes and 30 subprocesses regarding agency services and enabled them to provide 24/7 customer and agency service availability. It improved response time by almost 99% and even generated savings of more than 5% of total full-time equivalents. Not only that but, it increased the agency SLA success rate from 62% in 2018 to 96% in 2019 while the Net Promoter Score increased from -17 to +6. Digital Mirror ultimately increased the agency request quantity by 56% and created an additional $25 million premium production.

It also creates an innovation-centric culture that will expand the use of Digital Mirror to other business areas for overall improvement.

Expert Analysis by Laurent Fayet

Director Data & Analytics, BearingPoint

By providing a digital copy of a physical product or process(es), Digital Twin technologies give the ability to companies implementing them to identify pain points and improve their business performance. In a digitalized society, Digital Twin technology is deemed to grow in importance thanks to a wider range of applications and will benefit both companies performance and customer satisfaction.

The potential is gigantic but the reality behind the creation of Digital Twin should not be overlooked: this technology is data intensive. For a Digital Twin to be a mirror of a physical product or process(es), it can't be designed as an instant photograph. Like any organization, a Digital Twin is a living organism which requires a massive and constant feed of data to ensure the virtual representation is identical to the physical reality.

For that purpose, data ingestion, storage, processing, exploitation and consumption are critical components required to ensure the validity and representativeness of a Digital Twin. Over the past 20 years, all of these components have benefited from significant evolutions of concepts such as Big Data, real-time processing, digitalization, IoT, AI, etc. The ability to access, exploit and consume data has never been so important. Yet, the way data is managed, structured and governed is not always properly addressed, which creates risks as per the representativity of the Digital Twin.

To tackle this, a modern data management approach addressing the complete value chain is essential in providing a data ecosystem supportive of Digital Twin technologies. Such an approach will ensure the management of data assets and their necessary governance, evolving alongside the organization, assuring data quality and enabling an accurate representativity of data for live mirroring.

Companies creating Digital Twins should be careful not to focus only on the technological dimension but also ensure their data strategy is supportive of this approach to provide the right data ecosystem. If not, The Digital Twin will turn into a Digital Sibling who, even though issued from the same environment, will not be a true representation of the reality and will be of limited value in optimising business performance.

65: WEB TRAFFIC DATA DRIVES MARKETING ROI

#russia #asia #retail #analytics #advertising #devops
#cloud #customer #product #recommendation

Hoff is a Russian multibrand store retailing furniture and home goods in the hypermarket format. Founded in 2007, the Hoff company opened its first hypermarket in Moscow in 2009. Today, Hoff has 25 outlets across Russia and nine hypermarkets—four in Moscow, as well as Samara, Krasnodar, Rostov on Don, Voronezh, and Yekaterinburg. Its website sees over 12 million unique visitors annually. Hoff is Russia's only hypermarket retailer for furniture and household items, providing complete interior design solutions under one roof.

As Hoff's online presence grew, the company realized it needed to overhaul its online analytics which was quite patchy. The company wanted to know how its online and offline activities are connected, and the effectiveness of its marketing through the relationship between its online advertising and offline sales.

It needed Google Cloud Platform (GCP) to accomplish its objective. Hoff moved to overhaul its existing revenue attribution models and optimize its online marketing strategy. It partnered with OWOX to create a new end-to-end analytics system with Google Cloud Platform. OWOX and Hoff created a platform that could collect, analyze, and export the data simply and quickly by leveraging the power and ease of use of GCP). Using OWOX BI Pipeline, Hoff imported data from multiple sources into Google BigQuery, the heart of the new analytics platform.

With this solution, the company was able to put its new insights into practice. It was able to measure the effectiveness of its advertising on customer behavior. It discovered new ways to further increase sales. Hoff's online advertising return-on-investment increased by 17%. With the cloud-based infrastructure, the company was also able to save its resources on DevOps and IT support staff.

Expert Analysis by Dave Cherry

Executive Advisor at Cherry Advisory, LLC

Hoff's challenge is one that is common to retailers across the industry today—understanding and then influencing the relationship between online advertising/browsing and in-store sales. With the vast proliferation of customer journey permutations, it is a considerably daunting task to assign definitive attribution of an in-store sale to any digital activity. The challenge is complicated by the fact that most consumers engage and experience brands in various mediums and formats—email, text, video, social media, and more.

By leveraging GCP) and GBQ to collect and analyze vast quantities of data, Hoff was able to effectively make assumptions about the specific effectiveness of advertising on customer behavior and hence conversion. But was their online advertising ROMI actually 17%?

It's nearly impossible to know for certain, even when using coupon codes that provide a direct linkage from advertisement to conversion through redemption. Often consumers see the ad and transact but may not apply the code.

So, while there is more information available in a timelier manner to Hoff's analytics teams to make better marketing decisions, a more definitive efficiency is on the IT support side where the time savings can be more directly quantified. And through that value creation, the advertising ROMI is certainly increased.

66: Netflix "Watches" Subscribers While They Watch—To Give Them More to Watch

#usa #northamerica #streaming #media #entertainment
#recommendation #predictive #customer #analytics

Netflix is a California-based production company and entertainment service provider serving 180+ million paid subscribers in over 190 countries. Founded in 1997, Netflix offers documentaries, TV series, and feature films across an extensive selection of themes, genres, and languages.

The streaming giant has instantly become the crowd's favorite because it enables viewers to watch as much content as they want, anytime, anywhere, and using any internet-connected device. Viewers can also play, pause, and resume watching their preferred shows anytime, all which itself enriches the data that Netflix captures about them. It then uses this information to fuel its recommendation engine to suggest what customers will enjoy watching, thereby retaining them.

The smart recommendation engine has been truly helpful for boosting Netflix's original content. As the company started positioning itself as a content producer, more than just an entertainment distribution platform, Netflix wanted to use its predictive model to promote its original shows to subscribers who are fans of the US's best-selling TV series and films.

Through data analysis, the company can easily determine which content pieces are well received by their viewers, which titles are frequently watched, how often playback is made, and which ones gain good ratings. All these data gems are imperative to Netflix, enabling the company to create content similar or akin to the crowd-pleasers.

The platform's data infrastructure includes Hive, Hadoop, and Pig, along with the familiar business intelligence tools, like MicroStrategy and Teradata. Netflix also uses Lipstick and Genie, its own open-source tools and apps. And, like the rest of Netflix's core infrastructure, this all runs in the Amazon Web Services Cloud.

To date, the strategy of using Big Data and analytics to fuel Netflix's smart recommendation engine has been a great success. As a result, over 90% of Netflix members choose to engage with the platform's original content, further boosting customer retention rates.

Expert Analysis by James Taylor

CEO at Decision Management Solutions

Operations are central to this story—operations generate the data and operations consume the recommendation. Operational customer behavior is the engine of your analytics and the right place to apply that engine is in operations—not the executive suite! Make data-driven recommendations customer by customer.

Netflix has it easy here because success is easy to track—did you watch it and like it—and they get immediate feedback on recommendations. You won't be so lucky—it's harder to define success and it takes longer to see if your recommendations were good. To drive smart recommendations, you'll need to break down your recommendation decision and think about the pieces.

If you're trying to deliver smart recommendations in regulated industries like financial services, integrate rules-based compliance with data-driven insight as a single, compliant recommendation engine. Don't let these two pieces be developed separately!

67: Brewing Up a Latte Big Data Benefits

#usa #northamerica #coffee #restaurant #leisure #hospitality
#transaction #customer #personalization #ai #analytics #digital

Leveraging data and analytics may be an obvious strategy for many online businesses and digital services, like Amazon, Facebook, and Google. But for companies running physical brick and mortar stores, like Starbucks, it is not too evident how they take advantage of the power of data.

Starbucks does not only collect mounds of coffee beans to satisfy the coffee cravings of its customers; they also collect and leverage on the mounds of customer data to help them boost their performance and improve their customer's experience. With 25,000 stores worldwide, Starbucks makes an average of 90 million transactions weekly. This means the coffee giant has tons of data they can use to enhance their sales, marketing, customer support, and business decisions.

In 2008 and 2009, respectively, Starbucks launched its rewards program and mobile app, enabling the company to further collect customer's data and learn more about their buying behaviors. With 17 million customers using the mobile app, and 13 million customers benefiting from the rewards program, Starbucks is gaining an overwhelming amount of data and insights about what coffee their customers are buying, what stores are they buying from, and what time of the day, as well as information like weather, holidays, complimentary products, and special promotions. This enables it to improve customer experience and loyalty in a variety of ways:

- *Through the rewards program and mobile app, Starbucks can identify valuable information like their customers' preferred drinks and what time they usually order their coffee. With these data, the barista will not only be able to give them their preferred order, but they can also suggest new products that the customers are most likely to purchase.*

- *Starbucks uses what it calls a "digital flywheel program"—a cloud-based artificial intelligence program to recommend products to customers, even to those who don't even know what they want. The engine's sophistication is such that the recommendations can dynamically change depending on external factors, including weather, holiday, time of day, or the location of the customer.*

- *Because the system already knows what customer preferences and buying behaviors are, it helps the company to craft personalized offers and discounts. Additionally, using a customer's buying history, it can send customers who haven't been an active buyer emails to entice them to visit their nearest Starbucks.*

- *Starbucks' mobile app is programmed with an artificial intelligence algorithm that enables users to order their favorite drink as if talking to a virtual barista. With the different choices, preferences, even nuances, to a single order, the mobile app makes the order fast, easy, and seamless.*

- *Starbucks can quickly access which drinks and products are favored by their customers. This means that they can easily upgrade their menu based on customers' preferences and behavior. For instance, some Starbucks stores offer alcoholic beverages. Looking at available data, the company launched "Starbucks Evenings" on locations where they saw the highest alcohol consumption from customers.*

Expert Analysis by Danette McGilvray

Owner at Granite Falls Consulting, Inc., Management Consulting, and Author of *Executing Data Quality Projects: Ten Steps to Quality Data and Trusted Information*

Other organizations reading this success story might be tempted to focus in on the technology described ("Wow—a digital flywheel! I want one of those!") as the most important contribution to what Starbucks has accomplished. Of course, the sophistication of applying artificial intelligence can be a game changer.

Yet there are many aspects that must work together to get the rewards described. As mentioned, it is about the data, but high-quality data is required and that does not happen magically. For example, is the data an accurate representation of what is happening/did happen in the real world? Is the data itself being updated according to schedule and are we receiving it in a timely manner? Data quality issues often arise when data is integrated. Are we confident there are no duplicates in the customer data? As transactions and preferences for a customer are collected, are the suggestions being given to the right person, not a different person with the same name?

The complexity of the behind-the-scenes work often surprises an organization if they are not aware of the equal investments in data management, processes, training, change management, etc. required to make this work. Other organizations can reap the same benefits—if they go into it with their eyes wide open and realize they need more than technology alone to make it work.

68: CULTIVATING A KNOWLEDGEBASE FOR IMPOVERISHED FARMERS

#usa #northamera #farming #agriculture #food
#digitaltechnology #mobiletechnology #smartphone
#database #recommendation #user #monitoring

Hundreds of thousands of poor farmers in third-world countries are not only exposed to health risks and dangers but are also living on a financial knife's edge. Many of these farmers earn barely a dollar per day. Most of the time, their income is unstable and often at risk.

Because of the lack of accurate and up-to-date information, these farmers are not informed about when bad weather will wipe out their crops, what diseases might destroy their livestock, how they can properly care for their plants and animals, and how much should they be selling their produce in the market.

To help resolve these problems, Grameen Foundation, a US-based non-profit organization that primarily uses data and digital technology to address poverty in a scalable and sustainable way, launched the Community Knowledge Worker (CKW) initiative. Funded by the Bill & Melinda Gates Foundation, the CKW program involves Ugandan and Latin American farmers helping thousands of other poor farmers like themselves by providing accurate and real-time information using mobile technology. With accessible data, the program aims to help farmers improve their businesses and livelihoods.

The CKW initiative in Uganda and Latin America works by choosing farmers who will be part of the "community knowledge workers." The CKWs will be given smartphones that are connected to specially designed databases, giving them access to accurate, real-time information that they will in turn share to the other farmers in their remote communities. Some of the information they will receive from their mobile devices include weather reports, tips for planting crops, treating pests and diseases, caring for animals, and identifying fair market prices for their produce.

With the help of Grameen Foundation and its partners, the CKW initiative has provided access to accurate, timely information to thousands of farmers in Uganda and Latin America that improved their productivity, reduced risks, and boosted their livelihood. More than 62,000 poor farmers in Uganda have benefited through the help of mobile technology and services of more than 1,200 CKWs. At present, more than 300,000 farmers in remote communities continue to benefit from the CKW program through a wide network of thousands of peer advisors.

Expert Analysis by Mark Milone

Director, Global Data Strategy at Boeing, and attorney specializing in data governance, cyber security, and privacy compliance

Many organizations forget that access is only the first step towards effectively leveraging data. If you really want to get the most from data, then ongoing collaboration among data producers and data

consumers is necessary. The Community Knowledge Workers need a simple way to collaborate among themselves and with data sources. This collaboration will provide the context necessary to generate actionable intelligence from the data. For example, if the farmers could explain to data producers how they are using the data it is more likely that the data provided will fit their specific needs (i.e., the farmers should be able to generate requirements for the data).

If the farmers could agree on a structured format for generating these requirements, it will be easier for data sources to meet new, evolving needs. Also, the farmers should be able to escalate issues somewhere if the data is not of a sufficient quality, if access is denied at some point in the future, etc.

In essence, this program needs some kind of simple governance that increases the community's confidence in the data they use to make important decisions. Without a simple (but formalized) way of structuring the relationship between farmers and data sources, it will be difficult for this program to continuously improve and address new challenges that arise in the future.

69: Adding Some Fizz to Its Customer Loyalty Program

#usa #northamerica #beverage #drink #anlaytics #database
#marketing #consumer #fico #precisionmarketingmanager
#predictive #monitoring #loyalty #customer #cpg

The Coca-Cola Company is one of the biggest brand names in the world, with over a hundred years of history. Its huge product portfolio contains about 400 brands, including Coke, Sprite, Dasani, POWERade, Minute Maid, Costa Coffee, and a lot more, which are sold in almost every country around the globe.

The reason Coca-Cola carries hundreds of different beverage brands, with some of them similar to one another, is because the company believes that consumers in different locations, cultures, and life stages have unique and varying preferences. The company wants to give its customers an extensive selection of options to choose from.

The company's marketing team in North America decided to build stronger relationships with its loyal customers by launching a loyalty program where they can reward their devoted customers.

However, a one-to-one marketing effort may seem impossible, considering the company serves an average of 1.5 billion drinks daily.

Another challenge for the company's marketing team was coming up with interactive campaigns with a single touchpoint that would motivate their customers to join and engage with them. At the time, different brands were launching multiple campaigns due to the handling of different agencies. As a result, consumers became confused and developed separate relationships with individual brands. For instance, the same consumers who received a health newsletter from Diet Coke also might receive a discount coupon for their next purchase of Sprite. It was difficult for the company to understand their consumers' engagement behaviors across different touchpoints.

Coca-Cola developed a business case that would enable all brands to deliver engaging marketing content to their consumers through various channels, including web, mobile, and email. It then developed a system with intelligent analytics that captures, integrates, and analyzes consumer data from a wide variety of sources, implementing FICO's Precision Marketing Manager, a platform that applies predictive analysis to profile and segment consumers' behavior.

When the company launched its loyalty program called My Coke Rewards. Initially, the program included only three brands, Coke, Coke Zero, and Diet Coke. Within the first four months it included 13 brands, and in just 2 years, it has become the company's biggest loyalty marketing program, having acquired more than 11+ million active members.

The loyalty program is quite simple: The customer purchases any of the Coca Cola products, collects PIN codes from product packages and bottle caps, and then trades these codes for points. These loyalty points can be spent on rewards or be used as online contest entries at the My Coke Rewards website.

As more and more consumers engage with My Coke Rewards, this enables the company to use this increasing database of customer data to personalize campaign messages and offers. Moreover, the predictive analytics technology also helped the company identify the best actions to take with each individual consumer.

As a result, Coca Cola has acquired more than 11 million registered members through the My Coke Rewards program, with over 600 million PIN codes entered in the system. The traffic to the website has reached 8.6 million in the first year, and the company received more value out of its events sponsorship, including American Idol, NASCAR, and the Olympics. Above all these, the loyalty program strengthened the relationship of the brand with its customers, resellers, and business partners.

Expert Analysis by Dr. Kewal Dhariwal

CBIP, CCP, CDP, Co-founder of the Certified Data Professional (CDP) program, Co-founder of the Data Management Conference, and founder of the Microcomputer Institute

The Rewards solution illustrated by Coca Cola is an example of designing and implementing a program, learning quickly, adapting, and focusing on critical customer-behavior data. The key to success here is the utilization of an experienced strategic partner providing "tested and reliable" agile systems for analyzing and predicting recommended actions for diverse customer groups.

Since data lies at the base of all systems, this Rewards loyalty program is an illustration of a laser-focused CRM with extensive use of data analytics. Confirming if a marketing campaign has been effective is key to corporate success and decision making on future investments.

Gathering additional customer data from social media posts and photographs, etc., to be incorporated with customer satisfaction

surveys, along with retailer and wholesaler feedback will provide considerable insight. Streaming data analytics in real time is also very necessary to keep on top of today's ever changing "marketscape." Applications of machine learning, and predictive analytics will provide for intelligent automation of Coca Cola processes to speed up the company and allow it to compete even more aggressively with new products/services.

70: Adding Adword Analytics to Boost Online Marketing

#canada #northamerica #marketplace #ecommerce
#webanalytics #marketing #advertising #seo #adwords
#customer #recommendation #prescriptive #retail

Headquartered in Vancouver, British Columbia, BuildDirect is an online marketplace that specializes in heavyweight home improvement products. Focused on offering better-than-wholesale prices and excellent customer service, the company connects buyers with sellers of home materials, including flooring, roofing, decking, tiles, and so much more.

Founded in 1999, BuildDirect currently has a presence in over 100 countries in the world with a continuously growing portfolio. The company takes pride in being technologically-savvy, taking advantage of the Internet to grow their business and utilizing web analytics to continually improve their customer's experience.

Although the company's growth is outstanding, they wanted to improve their marketing campaigns and optimize their advertising spend as they have spent almost $1M only in the first year of their operation. The challenge was to identify which marketing strategies worked and which didn't, from a good mix of online subscription page, paid advertisements, and email newsletters. Additionally, they wanted to boost their ROI on the email marketing campaigns and reduce the abandonment rate of shopping carts from their website.

From their existing analytics tool, BuildDirect decided to move to Google Analytics, enabling them to get a bigger and better view of their online campaigns and modify them according to their desired goals. Google Analytics also helped them leverage on using long-tail keywords for their paid search campaigns, along with other features of the tool, including its Site Overlay and Defined Funnel Report capabilities. Having about 5,000 product SKU's, using long-tail keywords made their ads more targeted, driving customers to the right product page faster and with fewer clicks.

To further optimize their paid search campaigns, BuildDirect also linked their Google AdWords account with Google Analytics This decision helped them bring their AdWords strategies in house and dramatically reduce costs incurred by outsourcing from a third-party marketing agency.

All these changes helped BuildDirect boost their online presence and marketing performance. Using long-tail keywords resulted in a 37% increase in conversions, while taking advantage of the Site Overlay and Defined Funnel Report features of Google Analytics pushed them to simplify the payment process which then led to a 100% increase in sample orders.

Expert Analysis by Craig S. Mullins

President & Principal Consultant at Mullins Consulting, Inc.

Analytics projects must become more tactical and deliberate as business, and the economy as a whole, have become more digitized.

When it comes to optimizing marketing programs, specifically and accurately matching customer needs to your inventory will drive higher success rates. Today's consumers are used to being marketed to based on their specific needs and tastes, and tactics such as long-tail keywords as used by BuildDirect are crucial.

But even the most successful organizations and programs can encounter challenges that inhibit growth. Don't try to do everything at once when embracing a new analytics project. Assemble a reasonable set of measurable objectives that can deliver a quick return on investment. If you pursue too many goals at once it is easy to fall into a scattershot approach where none of your goals are met.

And after achieving initial goals, be prepared to adject and augment your analytics plans with incremental goals that add value. For example, BuildDirect could next seek to analyze market baskets to see which products are most frequently bought with others. Such an approach can sometimes deliver new insights that will modify the way products can be marketed in tandem, thereby increasing customer spend.

Additionally, a next step that BuildDirect can take would be to expand its marketing efforts to engage their customers on social media, which will open up an entirely new world of marketing data and metrics that can be used to grow their business.

71: Gee, GE Generates and Analyzes a Lot of Data

#usa #northamerica #aviation #healthcare #energy #manufacturing
#venturecapital #finance #machinelearning #ai #diagnostic
#recommendation #transaction #supplier #supplychain

General Electric (GE) has a highly diversified business and operating in eight major segments—aviation, digital industry, healthcare, power, renewable energy, additive manufacturing, lighting, and venture capital and finance.

From 2012, GE's profitability started to erode and the company underperformed the market. It had to initiate improvements, to make up for losses and gain recovery.

With an enormous volume of data across GE's business sectors. It is an immense challenge to organize and analyze it, let alone make intelligent use of it for financial and operational gains. Moreover, each operating unit has its own way of sourcing, purchasing and recording data about parts they purchase from suppliers. As a result, the same part purchased by different GE business units may be recorded with a different part number, description and other specifications. This means that GE corporate is unable to obtain the best pricing discounts.

To assist with this issue, GE utilized software from Tamr to help the company make sense of its massive purchasing processes and the immense, siloed data from them. The software's analytics and machine learning capability were able to clean hundreds of thousands of GE supplier records, eliminate inaccuracies, and multiple records from the same suppliers, making the data more usable.

GE now has an accurate and global view of its procurement data and found many opportunities for cost-saving and optimized spending. Just by consolidated purchasing of increased quantities from fewer suppliers, and leveraging this integrated and standardized data to renegotiate contract terms, GE saved $80 million in just a few years. Already it is working on more advanced analytics to reap improved procurement efficiencies and savings.

Expert Analysis by Jeremy Wortz

Cloud Engineer at Google, and Adjunct Professor, AI/ Tech Entrepreneurship, Northwestern University

GE's investment in an industrial IoT infrastructure is a key and costly decision many manufactures are faced with today. To enable the data-driven customer service, maintenance and overall use analytics use cases, a digital twin is needed to enable the analytics. By having end-to-end readings on the manufacturing, marketing, and merchandising aspects of the business, GE can simulate their entire operations using real-life data from every minute step of their processes.

These types of investments are large, costly, and span multiple years. To maintain momentum with this program, GE should focus on staged rollouts of the new infrastructure, focused on business

value by use cases. For instance, focusing on low hanging use cases such as a problematic product category that drives significant cost would be a great initial focus area for this use case. Even limiting the MVP to limited geographies can help to measure the lift of the overall investment. Once business value is understood of the use cases leveraged on-top of the infrastructure, the investment can continue to be rationalized and long-term momentum for large investments like this remain value focused and practical.

72: AI FOR AML, PDQ

#singapore #asia #banking #financial #venturecapital
#insurance #riskmanagement #ai #compliance
#customer #machinelearning #reporting #alerts

nited Overseas Bank (UOB) is a Singaporean multinational banking organization with headquarters in Singapore, with branches predominantly found in most Southeast Asian countries. It was founded in 1935 as United Chinese Bank (UCB) by Sarawak, Malaysia businessman Wee Kheng Chiang and was set up together with a group of Chinese-born businessmen. The bank, with 68 branches in Singapore and a network of more than 500 offices in 19 countries and territories in the Asia Pacific, Western Europe, and North America. It has a workforce of 26,000. UOB provides commercial and corporate banking services, private banking and asset management services, personal financial services, and venture capital, corporate finance, and insurance services.

UOB is a classic example of a financial institution using big data to drive risk management. Its data transformation journey began when it decided to adopt a data lake approach that involves consolidating data from all around the bank's different units into a central depository. It was quite a challenge with the bank's 80-plus years of history and data spread across its offices.

Among the earlier banks to introduce artificial intelligence for its compliance function. The challenge was to facilitate the sharing of algorithms across different geographical data sites without the need to share data itself that might otherwise breach customer privacy and data protection regulations.

Using AI, the bank was able to flag types of suspicious activity which were not possible to spot before with existing technology. Also, it was able to reduce the number of false positives or false alarms triggered by the stringent anti-money-laundering (AML) checks. Over the first six months of operation, the rate of false positives in name screening dropped by 60 % for individuals and 50% for entities. Over the same period, they achieve a 5% increase in alerts identified correctly as defined AML risks that otherwise would have gone unidentified. Risk analysis that initially took about 18 hours now takes only a few minutes.

UOB looks to build on this AI success by implementing intelligent solutions in other areas like credit decisions.

Expert Analysis by Gary Cao

Chief Data Officer, U.S. Venture Inc.

The United Overseas Bank (UOB) use case is an example of pattern detection, so that you can better identify any outliers (fraud, or money laundering activities). This story also demonstrates the advantage of data and technology over manual detection of outliers. Fraud is generally a low percentage of a huge volume of transactions with a high degree of complexity. ML/AI can perform much better and faster than experienced professional's manual research (with tips or leads, reasons for suspicion, narrowing down scope of specific research). Human brains cannot process anything with more than 3 dimensions, while AI/ML techniques can easily filter out unique activities with hundreds of attributes, and computing technology processing speed enable near-real-time scoring. Any similar "risk management" tasks can take advantage of such approach.

Some likely challenges for these kinds of projects: underlying data definition, standard formats, collection method consistency, and integration and aggregation of data. A more mature data technology infrastructure and long-term investment in this space would help overcome such obstacles. Other related opportunities in that industry: consumer or commercial lending credit risk prediction, or predictive targeting for prospects conversion to customers who may benefit from a niche product offering.

To take this kind of solution "to the next level": moving to near-real-time alert (within seconds of the transaction trigger), sharing the alerts with peer banks or regulatory/law-enforcement agencies, continue to refine and finetune the tools to improve accuracy, combining AI/ML alerts with top human experts in the space, designing multi-tiered approach based on amount/scale/customer segmentation, etc.

73: BETTING BIG AND WINNING BIG WITH BIG DATA

#usa #northamerica #gaming #dining #entertainment #retail #datadriven #customerservice #analytics #cloud #hadoop #customer #monitoring #recommendation #personalization #marketing

Caesars Entertainment is a global leader in gaming, hospitality, dining, entertainment, meetings & conventions, and shopping. The owner of some of the most iconic brands such as the Caesars Palace, Flamingo, Harrah's, and Horseshoe, it operates over 50 casinos, hotels and golf courses, 10 properties in Las Vegas, and other locations including Atlantic City and Macau, China.

The entertainment company boasts of having world-class facilities that include the following: the no. 1 & 2 theaters in the world, more than 200 nightlife venues, 39,000 rooms and suites catering to 15 million guests annually, 300+ restaurants and dining outlets, and meeting and convention centers able to accommodate 2 million attendees per year. The entertainment company has operations spanning four continents.

Caesars is a data-driven organization that uses data for its decision-making in every facet of the business, especially in its customer service and loyalty programs. It pioneered in the use of massive amounts of data in the early 2000s to support new marketing campaigns targeted at its customers.

More recently, the company implemented a new analytics engine that utilized Cloudera Hadoop and a cluster of Xeon E5 servers. It started applying analytics for its Gold Rewards loyalty program, which eventually evolved into the award-winning Total Rewards, now with 45 million members. The program adopts a data-driven and closed-loop approach in delivering a personalized experience for Caesars' guests. Members are tracked from the moment they book until the time they leave the hotel or casino. The data gathered is analyzed and used to provide top notch services to the members.

By making use of data on customer information and behavior, Caesars can quickly respond to important customer needs in a more personalized manner. Offers could be tailored and floor staff could be ready to greet customers and usher them to their favorite game. As customers spend more at gambling tables and resorts, Total Rewards gives away meals, room upgrades, tickets to shows, and limo rides to them. On a bad day at the casino, guests are surprised with gifts. Through these actions, Caesars can cultivate customer loyalty.

The results of this project have been spectacular. It increased the company's return on marketing programs. The data-driven approach has enabled Caesars to be able to trace 85% of its customer-related costs, up from barely 50% previously.

Expert Analysis by Joe Sommer

Managing Director, FSO Consulting, Data & Analytics, EY

Many companies talk about using technology, data and analytics to improve customer service and build loyalty, but Caesars has actually done it by investing in people, processes and programs. By gathering data from multiple touchpoints and channels, Caesars is able to offer targeted offers and rewards to suit individual clients. These enticements are an investment in the client relationship. Caesars' data analytics program increases the profitability of that spend by identifying the profiles of customers who will respond favorably to specific types of rewards. By collecting client data and their responses over time, their models become increasingly effective.

No doubt, there were some misses early on, both with the behavior forecasting and in applying big data technology. But Caesars stayed the course and learned from their efforts. They had people who were able to learn and were given the leadership support to invest in emerging capabilities. Now their loyalty program Total Reward is a mature business asset with detailed information on over 45 million clients. This asset is leveraged by over 200 data analysts and has proven its effectiveness in creating actionable insights about what rewards to offer specific clients to maximize their satisfaction—and Caesars profits.

74: AI AND BLOCKCHAIN GIVE
DRUG DEVELOPMENT
A SHOT IN THE ARM

#germany #europe #ai #technology #medical #biotech #daas
#machinelearning #AI #blockchain #datalibrary #cloud #document

*I*nnoplexus AG is a German technology company* that provides artificial intelligence (AI) systems that produce intelligence and insights for businesses such as pharmaceuticals, biotechnology, life science companies, and contract research organizations (CRO), which provide outsourced contract research service to those businesses. Founded in 2011 and headquartered in Germany, Innoplexus has offices in the United States and India. The company has over 250 employees in multidisciplinary teams and 20 global clients including many big pharma.

In the past, many businesses were unaware of the availability of vast data in the public domain. They were spending heavily on manually developed and curated products. They needed access to an automated system capable of managing large scale volumes of data and applying AI to capture relevant information.

Innoplexus offers Data as a Service (DaaS) and Continuous Analytics as a Service products that leverage Artificial Intelligence (AI) and advanced analytics to significantly reduce drug development time, from synthesis to approval. It provides a platform called iPlexus that automates the collection of billions of data points from thousands of sources using machine learning, network analysis, ontologies, computer vision, and entity normalization.

Ontosight, Innoplexus's life sciences data library, features search tools rooted in AI and blockchain technology. It was compiled to help researchers in the pharma and biotech fields sift through relevant data faster and streamline the drug development process. The massive repository is the largest data ocean on life sciences containing information from 1.3 million thesis and dissertations, to over 42 million published articles, 28.6million patents, and many other reliable sources.

Innoplexus deployed Google Cloud Platform (GCP) and is currently running 90% of its analytics on this platform to generate continuous intelligence and insights across different stages of drug development spanning the pre-clinical, clinical, regulatory, and commercial stages.

Innoplexus has reduced its analytics costs by 80% over its prior hosted physical infrastructures. The architecture has enabled Innoplexus to increase the number of life sciences content crawled from 1,000 to 20,000 pages per second. Moreover, its learning engine has accelerated training of information extraction models by a factor of 20 compared to similar services, and also supported an eightfold increase in scalability.

Expert Analytics by Eric Kavanagh

Co-founder and CEO, The Bloor Group, and
syndicated radio host of The Strategic CDO

"You, too, will be assimilated," said the algo to the text.

Turns out the written word can be quickly ingested, at breathtaking scale, to produce remarkably useful analysis of practically any topic. That's because the confluence of AI, blockchain, cloud and IoT is a crazy-big deal.

More than anything, what these ML/AI and blockchain solutions do is tackle the tedious. No human enjoys tedium, and in fact, it's probably the #1 morale killer in organizations today, especially scientific operations that require machine-like attention to detail.

By liberating the mind, solutions like Ontosight foster discovery, and that gets professionals excited. When you know you're onto something and the tools become transparent, you're in the zone of innovation. And when good things happen, everyone is happy.

75: Plenty of Room for Customer Analytics

#usa #northamerica #global #hotel #travel #hospitality
#monitoring #customer #automation #predictive
#datastrategy #forecasting #marketing

Marriott International is one of the largest hotel chains in the world with over 7,000 properties throughout 130 countries. Marriott has an inventory of nearly half a million rooms and continues to expand. Its customer loyalty program has grown to 120 million members around the world.

The hotel chain recognizes the value of innovation and understands how to use data to guide its business decisions. Revenue management and customer satisfaction are Marriott's main areas of focus. In pursuing its goals in these areas, the company uses data to track competitor brands and hotels and determine other sources of new revenue streams, such as new services and facilities. It ensures that their efforts satisfy both guests and the people in the local community.

In its revenue management, Marriott sets optimized prices to achieve the best possible profit margins. Its approach is known as

Dynamic Pricing Automation (DPA). DPA enables the hotel chain to accurately predict demand and patterns of customer behavior. It requires real-time, accurate data from a variety of sources including reference to global and local economic factors, events, and weather reports. It also factors in key metrics such as average daily rate, average occupancy rate, cancellation and occupancy, reservation behavior, and revenue and gross operating profit per available room.

With this information, Marriott can predict customer behavior and understand how its properties are performing relative to their competitors in the same area targeting similar profiles. And it can adjust its pricing strategy proactively.

Starwood Hotels, a Marriott subsidiary, started implementing the same approach two years ahead of merging with Marriott International. It invested more than $50 million in its Revenue Optimizing System (ROS), which can integrate data from both internal and external sources and suggest optimal prices based on the results of its real-time analysis and demand forecast, much similar to what Marriott does. The ROS) automatically adjust rates during low seasons. This dynamic pricing automation enabled Starwood to achieve a 5% increase in its revenue-per-room in one year, adding millions of dollars to its bottom line.

Expert Analysis by Evan Levy

Partner, Integral Data, LLC

Marriott and other players have had to continue to invest in analytics not to maintain a competitive advantage, but to keep up with the Online Reservation Industry players. What's different from the past is that the traveler now has access to that information too. There's a slew of internet sites that can provide pricing details, promotions, and ratings of nearly any hotel on the planet—all with only a few clicks—and free of charge.

The world of consumer marketing is ripe for innovation and disruption again — the evolution of consumer data protection laws and information privacy will inevitably create opportunity and carnage. I wonder if they'll evolve into other kinds of solutions such as:

- Licensing an individual's travel-related data. The consumer receives a fee for their data broker sharing their information with a travel related company

- Leap frogging the marketing, ad, and online reservation agency approach and using a crowd influencer model (e.g., Youtube, TikTok, etc.)

- True 1-to-1 personalized offers that create itineraries specific and unique to each traveler (based on personal, spouse, or family member preferences)

76: The Value of Data Alone Keeps Airlines Aloft During Covid Crisis

#usa #global #airline #travel #tourism #accounting #monetization #loan #lending #financial #customer #leisure

American Airlines, Inc. is the world's largest airline in terms of fleet size, revenue passenger mile, and passengers carried. It is headquartered in Fort Worth, Texas, in the Dallas-Fort Worth metroplex. On the other hand, United Airlines is another major American airline based at Willis Tower in Chicago, Illinois. It operates both domestic and international flights, and its route spans large and small cities across the US and all over six continents.

The Covid-19 pandemic has caused countless businesses to fall drastically, especially companies related to traveling. Even these two large airline companies, American and United, were not exempted from the pandemic's adverse effects. American and United were gravely stricken by the travel bans imposed in response to mitigating the spread of Covid-19 and were forced to collateralize data from their AAdvantage (American) and MileagePlus (United) customer loyalty programs for loans.

A few years ago, this action would not have been part of the options for these companies. Why? The reason can be rooted in antiquated accounting standards greatly influenced by the 1930's Depression Era. IFRS (International Financial Reporting Standards) and GAAP (Generally Accepted Accounting Principles) rules generally prohibit businesses from reporting and recognizing the value of their data. Before the dominance of computational methods, all data were physical. Up to now, amid the Informational Age, the real value of data is yet to be acknowledged entirely due to these archaic accounting rules.

The recent rise of proactive data appraisal gives data-savvy and data-rich businesses the ability to maximize their data assets for their gains. They wouldn't need to wait for emergencies to force them to utilize their customer data as a cushion for their fall, as what happened to Sports Authority and Radio Shack a few years ago. These pre-digital businesses were pressed into appraising their data only when they were in grave trouble.

Luckily for American and United airlines, they were able to realize the value of their customer data before the point-of-no-return. American Airlines was able to collateralize their customer data for a minimum of $19.5 billion to a maximum of $31.5 billion when the company's value was only at less than $8 billion. Similarly, United Airlines' customer data was valued at $20 billion, whereas its market cap was just $9 billion.

The proactive data appraisal of companies enables them to quantify the potential value of the customer data they hold. Failure to do so may lead to complacency in the way the data is managed, integrated, and maximized. In turn, this results in missed opportunities to utilize the data to generate previously unexplored economic benefits.

Expert Analysis by Doug Laney

Innovation Fellow, Data & Analytics Strategy, West Monroe | Professor of Infonomics, University of Illinois Gies College of Business

This story highlights and presages how data is and will grow in importance as a source of tangible capital. Investors and creditors today recognize the real value of data assets, despite the fact that antiquated and arcane accounting practices still do not. We know this, not only from this example, but from research that shows how data-savvy organizations (i.e. those with chief data officers, data science organizations and enterprise data governance functions) are command a 200% greater market-to-book value ratio than the market overall. And data-product companies have a 300% higher market-to-book value.

Like oil and real estate previously, commercial banks and investors tell us there's near infinite money chasing data-rich organizations. And innovative financial vehicles and accounting have emerged to capitalize on the "data gold rush." In fact, some companies have even "assetized" their data in the form of special purpose vehicles (SPVs) which are created as holding companies for the parent company's data. In this way the value of the SPV (if not the data itself) can be reported as a corporate asset. Accounting shenanigans? Perhaps. But who's going to argue that data has legitimate monetary value if a company's auditors sign-off on this kind of restructuring?

Moreover, some commercial banks are willing to fund data monetization efforts outright, putting data assets into a trust, developing data products, then paying the data owner a commission or a licensing fee. Business leaders foregoing these kinds of opportunities are foregoing an incredible opportunity to create new revenue streams and sources of value.

77: All Aboard the
Big Data Express

#usa #northamerica #transportation #travel #train #monitoring
#predictive #prescriptive #analytics #sensor #machinelearning #ai #rail

Norfolk Southern Corporation is one of the premier transportation companies in the U.S. It serves every major container port in the eastern United States and provides efficient connections to other rail carriers. Norfolk Southern (NS) is a major transporter of industrial products, including coal, chemicals, agriculture, automobiles and auto parts, metals, and construction materials. The railroad operates the most extensive intermodal network in the East.

A few of Norfolk Southern's biggest challenges in operating 19,500 miles of track are monitoring the health of its rail infrastructure and replacement of parts and supplies before they wear down or fail, including rail segments and locomotive batteries, and limited visibility into customer railcar demand.

In dealing with its issues, Norfolk Southern leveraged big data and analytics to improve its process that previously involved employing corrective actions after the problems occur. It made use of useful relevant information from existing data sources and more than 200 sensors recently installed on locomotive engines and more than 3,900 locomotives, which provide data through a machine learning-based model. Norfolk Southern also developed models that integrate data and perform transportation analytics to predict when preventive actions need to be done—well in advance of the anticipated issues. For example, curve track lubrication is improved. The new system also can predict shipment, fuel and power, network, and crew requirements up to ten days in advance. Workers can detect a loss of cooling water a week in advance and predict a dead battery a month ahead of time.

Norfolk Southern now identifies issues on the same day as it continuously optimizes and improves fleet management through analytics. Issues such as wear and tear on rail curves, cooling water leaks and locomotive battery failures can be predicted in advance with nearly 100% accuracy. Visibility into customer railcar demand improved from six hours to 10 days, a 3,900% improvement enabling the company to work towards its goal of developing train schedules that are reliable daily. The company forecasts $200 million in savings by enabling trains to run just 1 mph faster on average.

Expert Analysis by Randy Bean

CEO/Founder of NewVantage Partners, and
author of *Fail Fast, Learn Faster*

Big Data is transforming how companies do business. Norfolk Southern is a classic example. The transportation company is aggregating data from existing data sources and sensor devices to identify preventive maintenance needs. Norfolk Southern is combining the power of Big Data with AI, though machine learning models, to potentially save the company $200M.

Data initiatives that are driven by targeted business outcomes and busines-driven use cases are far more likely to succeed. Remember, it is not enough to build a data capability if there is not a compelling business need that can drive a successful outcome. Norfolk Southern should build on this initial success to identify new and additional business needs. Identify quick wins, establish credibility with results, create momentum. This is how companies become data driven.

78: CLINICAL PATHWAYS
PAVED WITH DATA

#usa #northamerica #healthcare #hospital #medical
#machineintelligence #machinelearning #ai
#automation #customer #recommendation

Mercy is one of the US's largest healthcare systems with 43 acute care and specialty hospitals, 40,000 workers, more than 700 physician procedures and facilities, and over 2,000 physicians in Arkansas, Kansas, Missouri, and Oklahoma. Mercy has earned second place in the annual Healthcare Informatics Innovator Awards as Healthcare Informatics magazine recognized the institution for its Clinical Pathways program that identified hidden care variation patterns through the facilitation of an artificial intelligence-based application.

Before the launching of Mercy's Clinical Pathways program, their original approach involved provider groups, who were under escalating pressure while transitioning to value-based payment models, which resulted in the vulnerability to bias and incompetent lack of buy-in. Mercy decided to adopt a new process that was efficient and backed by their own data—the Ayasdi Care platform.

The Clinical Pathways program enabled Mercy to leverage machine-learning, and geometric algorithms to refine clinical pathways through artificial intelligence and massive-data methodology facilitated by Ayasdi. The application adopted by the program also had the ability to fast-track care model development by extracting clinical and patient data directly from Mercy's integrated systems of record. Ultimately, Mercy's new insights-driven pathway program cut back 5% off knee replacement costs while enhancing the quality and maintaining low mortality and morbidity rates across all cases.

Results from the Clinical Pathway program by Mercy made waves in the health system for the big-data breakthrough that reduced healthcare discrepancy in costly procedures. The outcomes drawn from this initiative include the development of 30 optimal clinical practice pathways at a significantly faster pace, and a first-year savings of $14.7 million, and $9.4 million savings the subsequent year. It also significantly reduced the average length of stay for knee replacements from 3.3 days to just 2.4 days. And through a data-backed procedure that pushed clinician adoption, it enabled more focus on patient care due to increased free time.

"This award underscores the unique capabilities that artificial intelligence and big data offer to healthcare organizations in their pursuit of delivering the highest-quality and most cost-efficient care for their patients," said Dr. Gurjeet Singh, Ayasdi CEO, as he highlights the gratification that comes with taking big leaps in the healthcare industry that translates to increased care quality and more lives saved. Mercy looks to deploy over 50 more clinical pathways over the next few years.

Expert Analysis by Bryan Komornik

Partner, Healthcare Payer Strategy & Solutions at West Monroe Partners

The first thing that stuck out to me was how early the data-centric effort engaged and incorporated the perspectives external providers and stakeholders. This is a critical success factor, paired with a strong communication and training strategy, for all engagements when you want to create sustainable and measurable change. The successes and outcomes may create an opportunity for Mercy to take what they've learned and use it as a feedback loop to educate med students, residents and others in the spirit of preparing the next generation of leaders.

Another thing to note within the case is the pattern utilized to measure success was primarily for elective procedures. It makes sense to start as these are high cost, and often avoidable, however there is additional opportunity for Mercy to expand the data set to include other settings, practices and procedures / underlying conditions. It would be valuable for Mercy to evaluate and potentially refresh its analytics to remove unintended and unconscious biases. Moving forward, Mercy may further consider utilizing their AI and creating a broader data-share with other systems and health plans to improve engagement and outcomes, keeping the patient/member in focus at all times.

79: The 9-1-1 on IoT Data

#usa #northamerica #medical #healthcare #emergency #iot
#monitoring #alerting #customer #government
#emergency #police #fire

RapidSOS is a US-based privately funded company engaged in the emergency services platform business. It has partnered with IoT companies and the public safety community to create the RapidSOS Emergency API — a product that links any connected device to 9-1-1 and first responders, making it possible to get unprecedented life-saving data to public safety in an emergency.

One of the most pressing challenges of the public safety community in recent decades has been obtaining an accurate location for mobile 9-1-1 callers. With the legacy 9-1-1 infrastructure, tracing accurate caller locations of mobile device users fast is difficult causing unnecessary delays in making the response possible.

One of the major products RapidSOS offers to the market is its RapidSOS NG911 Clearinghouse. It works either with a response center's existing software or by way of a web application. In 2018, RapidSOS was developing its Emergency API. The company had an existing platform that was receiving signals from the outside and processing them. Its use was customized for each client. A more intuitive module for the interface that enables users to design workflows on their own interactively and graphically was needed to serve more clients quickly.

In the course of utilizing Rapid framework to design the solution, RapidSOS service providers had to extend the capabilities of the framework and develop one of its functionalities for its new version. The module worked and there was no further need to customize the process for each user.

Apple, Google, and Uber partnered with RapidSOS and integrated RapidSOS's technology to provide 9-1-1 response centers with more useful data such as a user's location and diagnostic details that can help determine the kind of response action needed.

To accelerate the deployment of the RapidSOS Next-Generation-911 Clearinghouse, Microsoft Ventures joined RapidSOS in a $16M funding round in April 2018.

The RapidSOS Emergency API Suite provides various APIs to send data from any IoT device or app directly to 9-1-1. This product is now used by 250 million users and over 3,500 public safety agencies nationwide receiving data from hundreds of millions of devices through RapidSOS and saving lives every day.

Expert Analysis by Tony Almeida

Founder, Blue Dragon Consulting LLC

Both public and private safety services can benefit from this solution as it enables both the user' location and diagnostic details that can help determine the kind of response action needed. This solution creates a learning engine for a more effective action for each specific situation. For a wider adoption it is critical that the platform uses open source for the API enhancements and no code for the front-end application.

Initiatives that leverage emerging technologies such IoT when combined with a machine learning engine can enable solutions that can be adopted by several industries. For instance, it could enable the tracking and location of cars, trucks, trailers, cargo, etc. Both financial and insurance companies can leverage the solutions to reduce loss, mitigate risk through the leverage of analytics in near-real time, as well as to create models that support underwriting. The monetization of this solution investment is fully returned by other industries adoption, as well as by the products impact in loss mitigation of both lives and assets.

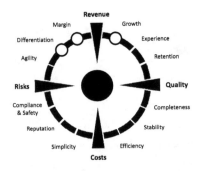

80: Expressing How to Increase Revenue by Monetizing Store Data

#usa #northameria #gasoline #oil #energy #retail
#transaction #reporting #customer #monetization

Express Mart is a private American company that operates a 78-chain of gasoline stations with convenience stores, employs over 500 staff throughout New York State

With New York being a highly competitive market, Express Mart was seeking ways to drive revenue. With the fast-paced rise of digital commerce, the brick-and-mortar retail segment and convenience channel have struggled to drive greater foot traffic. The store chain tried to leverage revenue improvement in a different way—from the supply side.

To execute its strategy, Express Mart engaged Skupos, data analytics specialists, and the largest third-party provider of scan data solutions for the convenience store industry. Skupos records billions of transactions at the point of sale every year from thousands of stores to provide key suppliers with scan data reporting in exchange for refunds that go back to the retailer. Its data analytics tools assist thousands of stores all over the US.

The technology enables stores to get paid for scan data. They also gain access to cheaper product pricing through discount programs that are similar to that of larger convenience store chains. The sales insights benefit vendors but the cash flow from supplier to the retailer via Skupos was one of the major wins for Express Mart.

Express Mart experienced a sudden monthly revenue increase of 16%. Additionally, what typically took several hours each week to format and export its transaction data for IRI now takes less than an hour for the entire 78-store setup. Express Mart can now see all vital information in a centralized dashboard to ensure a clear view of company-wide performance.

Expert Analysis by Alice Huang

Senior Manager, Data Engineering and Analytics, West Monroe Partners

This is something that resonates with brick-and-mortar stores nationwide. With the rise of e-commerce cutting into the market, brick-and-mortar stores everywhere are getting squeezed.

Express Mart reacted to this seismic shift by pivoting in such a way that achieved two goals with one initiative. Express Mart recognized and leveraged the monetary value living within their data warehouses. Furthermore, by automating their data collection processes, they set themselves up to scale efficiently in the future, thereby reducing the cost of growing their business.

Express Mart's vendors also benefit from their knowledge. With additional insight into how customers truly spend their money, vendors can better position themselves for competition in the market and for future customer trends.

Win-win solutions like these are not easy to find. With the introduction of a savvy data-based solution, Express Mart and its vendors demonstrate how mutually beneficial "co-opetition" helps everybody make it through seismic market shifts. Going forward, both Express Mart and their vendors can start exploring value creation opportunities by leveraging the data they amass.

81: CASHING IN ON MACHINE LEARNING

#spain #europe #banking #financial #lending #analytics #transaction
#machinelearning #riskanalysis #customer #reporting

C aixaBank, S.A. is the parent company of a group of financial services companies. It is Spain's third-largest lender, with over 5000 branches and 9000 ATMs to serve its 16 million customers.

Wire banking is prominent between countries throughout the EU and beyond, and most of its competitors are going 100% digital. Therefore, Caixa Bank needed a strong infrastructure across digital channels if it wanted to retain its leadership spot in the marketplace.

Caixa Bank deals with a massive network of physical branches and has a significant number of international transactions. The solution had to be scalable for future volumes and growth, meet existing and future regulations regarding security and other guidelines, and able to handle data from multiple sources like commercial, retail, and internal, research to enable unified and consolidated access.

With machine learning capabilities from Oracle, Caixa Bank saw results quickly across the board in a number of processes. In the past, textbook derivation models were used for standard processes such as risk analysis for loan grants. It was transformed with machine learning powered by sophisticated algorithms. The results included a 7% accuracy improvement in models, which translated to a 12% increase in profits on loans.

In addition, Caixa Bank employees spend hundreds of thousands of hours at individual branches on complex processes such as performing oversight on utility payments made by clients through its banks. It developed and deployed an algorithm trained from thousands of historical decisions that resulted in a 99% accuracy match to human decision-making. By streamlining the processes, Caixa bank projected that 60,000 hours of human effort were saved across all branch employees from efficiency improvement, enabling them to spend more time on value-added tasks such as financial advisory, selling products and services, and other activities.

Expert Analysis by Nina Evans

Associate Professor, Professorial Lead: UniSA STEM
at University of South Australia (UniSA)

Advancements in technology allow much larger quantities of data to be processed and this case illustrates how efficiency improvement (operational excellence) can be achieved through implementing machine learning in Caixa, a large bank in Spain. Despite the attractiveness of new technologies such as machine learning to increase operational efficiency, the focus should remain on the business, not the technology per se.

The case study shows that most of Caixa's experienced a burning platform to digitally transform, as their competitors were 'going 100% digital' to support wire banking between countries. Customer expectations have also changed; they are more entitled and demanding and need to be more effectively engaged at every touchpoint in the customer experience lifecycle. A single digital platform is the best way to create a positive, personalised, straight-through, automated experience where customers can communicate across multiple digital channels (e.g. via mobile phone, web sites, social media, etc.). The digital platform actually 'becomes the business'.

Digital business transformation requires an amplified focus on data management. The case states that the bank needs to 'move into the world of big data and analytics. During research interviews conducted by the University of South Australia and Experience Matters (an information management consulting firm), a staff member from one of the big four banks in Australia commented: "We are actually a data management organisation, with a banking license." Data are therefore a bank's major assets, coming from multiple sources with varying quality.

The case shows how business processes have to be simplified and streamlined. In a banking environment, business processes such as risk analysis for loan grants can be powered by sophisticated algorithms and machine learning, leading to an improvement in accuracy of models and an increase in profits on loans. For complex processes requiring a large degree of decision-making, such as performing oversight on utility payments made by clients, an algorithm can be developed and trained from thousands of historical decisions to be at least as accurate as human decision-making.

Apart from the learning from the case description, it is important that organisations understand that they need an enterprise-wide transformation to keep up with competition and changes in their customers' expectations. This does not simply require a continuous process improvement program or a particular department overhaul. To remain viable in their industry, organisations must digitally transform their entire enterprise. Organisations that do not digitally transform will not survive.

Organisations have to develop solutions that are scalable, to create a future that is going to be sustainable, flexible, and agile enough to keep up with the pace of change in the environment; regulatory, system and technology changes, as well as worldwide events such as pandemics and natural disasters.

Organisations don't exist in a vacuum; they are part of an ecosystem with both upstream and downstream partner organisations such as government departments, charities, or regulatory bodies. For example, banks must comply with existing and future regulations regarding security and other guidelines.

As a consequence of digital transformation, people's jobs are impacted. People's skills and experience, i.e., employees who understand how the organisation works and who understand the customer base, products and services, are now more valuable than someone who merely understands the process. Having people who are loyal, engaged and passionate about the organisation is key to a successful business transformation.

Finally, an important prerequisite for digital business transformation is that it must be driven by the CEO and implemented by a dedicated team of executives (often led by the CDO), who take a holistic approach to transform the entire company. Digital business transformation is not a project or activity and should not be delegated to the CIO, CTO or CMO in isolation.

82: Flying High with Big Data-Supported Customer Relationship Management

#usa #northamerica #airline #flight #travel #transportation
#crm #loyalty #customer #recommendation #alerting

Delta Airlines is a major American airline headquartered in Atlanta, Georgia. It started operation in 1924 as an aerial crop-dusting operation. The airline serves nearly 200 million passengers yearly with 15,000 daily departures including flights operated by its partners. Delta's global network offers service to more than 300 destinations in 60 countries on six continents. It has 10 major hubs, 7 of them domestic and 3 are international.

Some of the major threats to Delta's business growth include the declining number of business flyers, the highly competitive market, and customers' desire for more personalized service, which is essential to gain customer loyalty.

Delta invests to drive innovation and projects for a more sustainable, growing business. It invested in big data to support its customer relationship management (CRM) program focusing on

255

enhancing loyalty and expansion of customers through more personalized services. The airline attributes its consistent annual revenue increase over the years to these factors; they have to be improved if they need to sustain their sound business position.

Delta Airlines creates value propositions based on increasingly real-time information about customer preferences and needs. It pieces together customer information like demographic profile, travel habits, and spending ability and makes use of more advanced data in its efforts to tailor promotions and better engage customers and generate loyalty.

Delta has also invested over $100 million in airport baggage systems with advanced tools for baggage data collection and analysis. In the past, connecting bags were being sent through the airport's luggage sorting system, which was time consuming and a non-value-added process. The system now automatically alerts baggage handlers when connecting bags need to be transferred directly to another plane.

Big Data has been aiding Delta Airlines to enhance CRM over the years; this has helped in customer loyalty and expansion and continues to sustain the airline's profitability and growth. It reported that an increasing number of passengers are choosing to go directly to delta.com over searching for airfare through an online travel agent like Orbitz or Kayak. A whopping 60% of its ticket revenue now comes from its SkyMiles members, and it saw a 35% boost in mobile platform revenue origination in 2019.

And by integrating real-time flight data into its baggage systems, Delta has optimized its process and is better able to identify key causes and trends in mishandled bags and implement effective solutions immediately.

Expert Analysis by Claudia Imhoff

CEO Intelligent Solutions, co-author of five books, and
founder of the Boulder BI Brain Trust (BBBT)

The airline industry has had a rough couple of years — this on top of other years of declining revenues and extreme competition between airlines. Delta Airlines is well aware of its current marketplace and is driven to get ahead of its competitors by focusing on the processes that directly impact their customers.

Generating customer loyalty means the airline must truly understand who their customers are, how their travel is changing, how their spending is changing, and solving nasty little problems — like lost luggage — quickly. That takes a lot of fresh, current, customer-specific data. The best example in this case study of their analytical prowess is in their baggage handling systems. There is nothing more frustrating to a traveler than to stand at the luggage conveyor belt until it stops, forcing the traveler to realize that their bags didn't make it ... It happens all the time. Informing a customer of the problem almost as soon as it happens (when the plane takes off without your luggage!) and having a solution when the plane lands goes a long way toward improving customer loyalty.

Bravo Delta for taking on this massively annoying problem in your quest to make the customer happy. Their solution should be adopted by all other airlines. I look forward to the day when all passengers get immediate feedback and solutions for other problems like missed or cancelled flights, fare changes, overbooked flights, maintenance problems, and other traumas for the flying public.

83: ROARING TO BOX OFFICE SUCCESS THROUGH DATA ANALYTICS

#usa #northamerica #media #entertainment #leisure #customer
#biotech #personalization #modeling #forecasting

The Walt Disney Company, founded in 1923, has businesses that include parks and resorts, media networks, studio entertainment, and consumer products, and interactive media.

Although Disney started to rely heavily on analytics over 10 years ago, it continues to explore its many applications across some of its business units. It is continuing to ramp up its investment in data analytics to improve the customer experience mainly for consumer and guest experience across its parks and resorts to give them the best possible visit. Disney's analytics team is largely consisting of staff and suppliers working on analytics-related tasks from data punching to face recognition.

The company's solution integration group leads the way in using analytics and technology in helping personalize the customer's Disney experience. It also played a leading role in The Lion King's Broadway success.

Lion King was staged in a smaller theater and had a shorter run compared to other popular shows. One of the areas Disney focused its analytics on to gain box office success is pricing and revenue management. The company harnessed big data technology effectively. It developed a dynamic pricing model for the show tickets to accurately forecast future demand for Lion King. It made use of historical Broadway ticket sales data. The model also predicted the highest possible price for each ticket that customers were likely to accept.

Analytics helped The Lion King generate more ticket revenue—about $8 billion—than any other Broadway show. It is the highest box office revenues in Broadway history by far.

The dynamic pricing model Disney developed for the show tickets will continue to be enhanced to hope to replicate Lion King's unprecedented success.

Expert Analysis by Iván Herrero Bartolomé

Chief Data Officer, Intercorp

The first thing of this story that captured my attention is the statement that the Disney's analytics team focuses its efforts in two key areas: improving the customer experience for their clients and increasing the profitability of the company. There is no doubt every analytics leader should have these two dimensions as the main railroads of its strategic roadmap.

Another interesting fact of this particular use case is that Disney's analytics team used external data (Broadway ticket sales data) to forecast the demand for Lion King, instead of being kept back by "we don't have data" or "that data won't work for us" kind of thoughts. Now that they know how the demand responded to each price for Lion King, they will be able to blend internal and external data to improve the accuracy of their dynamic pricing model, building on a virtuous cycle: using data to drive value, generating more data during the process, which can then be used again to drive more value, and so on.

As a final thought, I would like to highlight the importance of assembling a specialized, multiskilled team to deliver on sophisticated projects such as the one featured in this story. And then, treating these capabilities as a core corporate asset, leveraging them where the highest value can be achieved. Doing this at a company level is hard enough but scaling up and prioritizing these analytical capabilities at a conglomerate of companies, such as Disney or Intercorp, is a permanent challenge. If this is your case, my humble advice is the following: start small, prove value, build trust, get traction at some companies, start a movement, instill data fluency across the top management, scale up your team and then, start decentralizing, giving each company a clear direction and switching over the responsibility of execution to them.

84: Mapping Health Issues to Steer Community Education

#usa #northamerica #medical #healthcare #hospital
#businessintelligence #analytics #gis #geographic
#demographic #diagnostic #monitoring

T*he Children's National Health Services* is a Washington, D.C.-based healthcare center. It is ranked the top 7 children's hospitals in the country by U.S. News & World Report. Established in 1870, the hospital provides a wide range of pediatric care services including, cardiology and cardiac surgery, neurology and neuro-surgery, oncology, neonatology, orthopedic surgery, and sports medicine, among others. With a 323-bed capacity, the hospital has a prenatal pediatric institute, as well as a rare disease institute.

The CNHS has been advocating injury prevention, especially for children. Medical Teams offer injury prevention advice to residents of nearby communities to keep kids out of harm's way.

While the healthcare center's business intelligence and clinical analytics has done a good job of implementing a strong analytics program, Children's National Health System has not been very successful in focusing its campaigns on the real hotspots where health injuries occur, hence campaigns had not effectively targeted the right segments.

CNHS took its existing electronic health records system and integrated it with geo-spatial software from Esri. The new geographic information system (GIS) component enabled the center's analytics to display health data with geo-spatial coordinates. Pediatric burn cases were one of the first projects they focused on.

GIS) mapping enabled CNHS to identify the hot spots where injuries were occurring and map them out. The visual map-enabled staffers to devise prevention programs tailored to the demographics of areas with high rates of injuries. The staff worked with the community groups the system identified as having a cluster of toddlers with bad burns. If the high incidents of burn injuries occur in a Hispanic neighborhood, they would work with community groups to provide parents of young children with Spanish-language information about safety.

Today, Children's National Health System is seeing fewer burn patients overall and fewer patients requiring high-level burn care. With the Esri capability that gave CNHS's data analytics system mapping features, the staff now better understands what happens outside the four walls of their hospital to better prevent disease and conditions. Recently, Children's National is using the technology to map concentrations of other important medical conditions it is dealing with, such as obesity and asthma.

Expert Analysis by Adam Gersting

Senior Partner and Dallas Technology Lead, West Monroe

This is a great example of how richer insights can be gained by folding in another layers of data. Like ingredients into a sauce that one is "seasoning to taste," fold in one more spice and sees how the sauce tastes. Some new ingredients won't change the overall taste. Some will cause the whole sauce to taste like the new ingredient. Some additions will work greatly with what is already in the bowl and bring the whole sauce to life. This example shows how "folding in" the geo-location brought the overall "sauce" to life. With this additional insights, more targeted insights and steps can be taken. A consideration as well as opportunity around more granular customer data is the aspect of privacy. For example, teaming with telecom providers, there may be ability to determine individual persons and persona groups—to be able to reach out to via text or mobile avenues and gain more insights about. This could be highly valuable, although it would raise additional data privacy considerations.

85: SMALL CHAIN USES BIG DATA METHODS TO DRIVE CUSTOMER VISITS

#usa #northamerica #restaurant #dining #food #pos #customer #loyalty #monitoring #automation #analytics #hospitality

Fig & Olive is a chain of high-end Mediterranean specialty restaurants with sites in New York, Washington, D.C., and Los Angeles. Owned by Luxury Dining Group, Fig & Olive's mission is enhancing life's simple pleasures by offering an innovative approach to the classic French Riviera dining experience. The upscale restaurant group has several locations across the United States.

Fig & Olive finds the management and operation of an upscale restaurant group challenging. Attempting to combine the data from multiple restaurant locations into a centralized reservation center was even more difficult and particularly frustrating. The cost associated with combining the restaurant group's data from OpenTable, a real-time online reservation network for fine dining restaurants, and those from a Micros point-of-sale (POS) system in all its different locations across the US is daunting. So, Fig &

Olive's technology and information systems group searched for more feasible solutions.

At the time they were moving to a centralized reservation center, the restaurant group eventually chose Venga to power its guest management system using data from POS and reservations systems. In addition to combining the databases from its nine locations, Fig & Olive's ultimate goal is to use the new Venga system to increase customer satisfaction and loyalty.

Fig & Olive's guest management system was set up to match reservations to POS data. It enables the company to track guests' dining habits and visit frequency. This information it gets is then used to run automated marketing campaigns. In its "we miss you campaign," the restaurant group tried to woo back guests who had not visited in the last 30 days by offering complimentary crostini to them. Venga also privately solicited Fig & Olive guests' feedback through online surveys. It then sent guests branded "thank you" emails with feedback surveys the day after their visits.

According to Venga's data, the campaign resulted in 300 visits and more than $36,000 in sales, which was seven-times more than the entire cost of the program itself. The guest management system also significantly helped in improving customers' impression of the restaurant group. Fig & Olive negative reviews on Yelp decreased 36%.

Expert Analysis by Tim Wrzesinski

Technology Practice Director, West Monroe

We work with many clients, often with decentralized business units. A known tradeoff of decentralization is improved entrepreneurship for decreased standardization. We've found that centralization of data works best. Data is a shared asset, and requires a certain amount of centralization, multi-disciplinary collaboration across business units and standardization to be efficient. Finding the right balance of standardization and flexibility is critical to improving insights and deriving value from data, while not stymieing creativity.

Fig & Olive has centralized and standardized data through Venga, to create a Customer-360 experience, and has only started to scratch the surface of the benefits. Like Fig & Olive, we see many of our clients sitting on a wealth of customer data, yet to be integrated into a cohesive view and leveraged. But companies are waking up to the significant advantages of pulling Customer data together, marrying it with external data, and applying advanced models to improve customer experiences, customer retention and ultimately revenue. Fig & Olive is early on the journey but headed in the right direction. Laying out a roadmap of use cases with carefully measured anticipated value, is the next step to compounding their success.

86: Proactively Preventing Patients from Passing Away with Predictive Analytics

#usa #northamerica #healthcare #medical #hospital #patient
#monitoring #alerting #modeling #predictive #analytics #ai

Kaiser Permanente is an American integrated managed care consortium, based in Oakland, California. Kaiser has over 12 million health plan members and operates 39 medical centers and 690 medical facilities in eight US states and the District of Columbia. Kaiser Permanente is one of America's leading health care providers and not-for-profit health plans.

Kaiser Permanente's Research groups wanted a proactive approach on patients outside of the intensive care units but unexpectedly deteriorated in the hospital and immediately got transferred to the ICU. These patients generally have far worse outcomes than patients who are admitted to the ICU directly. Data and literature show that non-ICU patients that require unexpected transfers to the ICU make up only 2–4 % of the total hospital population. However, they account for 20% of all hospital deaths.

Their average hospital stays are also longer than other patients by 10 to 12 days.

Researchers at Kaiser started to analyze decades of medical information generated by the institution's integrated model and its electronic health system. The team, consisting of members from different groups within the consortium, developed a proprietary system of algorithms that monitors patient data and issues alerts for high-deterioration risk scores of non-ICU patients likely to deteriorate within the next 12 hours.

The team synthesized data from 650,000 patient hospitalizations and 20,000 deterioration cases across Northern California that included vital statistics, lab results, and other variables to train the system. New models were developed now and then to include improvements and clinical and operational workflows were implemented.

The system, named Advance Alert Monitor (AAM) system, is fully operational in all 21 medical facilities in Kaiser Permanente's Northern California region. AAM leverages three predictive analytic models to analyze more than 70 factors in a given patient's electronic health record to generate a composite risk score. Implementing the workflows enables health care teams to respond as efficiently as possible to alerts.

In its first two years of being operational, the program helped the health system reduce mortality by 20%. Kaiser Permanente's plan includes iterations of the program to integrate artificial intelligence.

Expert Analysis by Meta Brown
Associate Professor of Economics at The Ohio State University

The moral of the story might be that predictive models solve business problems, or that analytics is just for organizations that employ big teams of researchers, whatever "researchers" may be, or that a big repository of historical data is the key, and those without are left behind. These are common reactions to success stories, all too simple and none healthy. It's better to push beyond the story and ask how it really happened.

What, specifically, did Kaiser Permanente management do before, during and after this story? Why choose this particular problem for analysis? What actions and analysis took place before this particular project began, and what were the results? What exactly is a workflow, and how did management create and implement it? Who runs what in this system? What went wrong that nobody's mentioning? Ask questions and seek out the practical challenges and opportunities that are relevant to your own workplace.

87: No More Est. for ETAs Saves Millions

#germany #europe #airline #travel #passenger #customer #predictive
#digitization #automation #datascience #rapidminer #modeling

Lufthansa is the largest German airline and the largest airline in European terms of fleet size and passengers. The Lufthansa Group is a globally operating aviation group with more than 550 subsidiaries and affiliated companies. The company portfolio consists of network and point-to-point airlines and aviation service companies. Some of the aviation-related companies it owns are Lufthansa Technik, for aircraft maintenance services; AirPlus, involved in corporate business travel payment solutions; and LGBS which deals with finance, human resources, and purchasing for companies.

Lufthansa Industry Solutions, a Lufthansa consulting firm that provides services to both within the Lufthansa family and outside companies, provides digitizing and automation services for its clients' processes. The RapidMiner user group is a part of the consulting firm's business that helps to apply data science to a variety of problems and opportunities that include the use of RapidMiner.

Lufthansa's challenges predicting its departing aircrafts' arrival times was hurting its operational efficiency. When its plane arrives late at its destination, it brings inconvenience to passengers, may impact its catering service, movement of crews between aircraft, availability of gate, connecting flights of passengers, and many other concerns. All these contribute to additional costs for Lufthansa especially when a passenger misses a connecting flight.

The Lufthansa Industry Solutions project team put together a large and diverse data set that the team felt will have valuable predictive power. It consisted of profiles of previous flights and added other information such as weather data, radar data, and other related factors.

RapidMiner enabled the team to easily prep the voluminous data set for modeling. It resulted in better arrival predictions than what was previously available, with the actual arrival time of flights to within a 5-minute window, made at the very moment the planes took off. Such accurate predictions enable the Lufthansa operations team enough time to make necessary adjustments at the arrival destination, minimizing passenger inconvenience, and even the airline's cost, saving the company tens of millions of dollars.

Expert Analysis by John R. Talburt

PhD, CDMP, IQCP, Professor of Information Science and Acxiom Chair of Information Quality, University of Arkansas at Little Rock, and Lead Consultant for Data Governance and Data Quality Management, Noetic Partners

I find it amazing a company can save tens of millions of Euros using its own data and free software! The Lufthansa story reinforces a paradigm reversal that has been underway for the past few years. There is a major shift from software development and large, in-house computer systems as the key drivers for competitiveness to a new approach based on data-driven solutions in a world where software is rapidly becoming a commodity. The Big Data revolution ushered in by Hadoop map/reduce has changed the IT landscape in dramatic ways, perhaps most importantly the abundance of high-quality, open-source software and cloud computing. With the technology playing field leveled, companies are realizing their data are their unique resources and foundation of their competitive advantage in the marketplace.

The trend toward open-source software has not gone unnoticed by the education community. Always starved for resources, most information science and technology courses are now being taught with free tools such as RapidMiner, Weka, Knime, Python, and Spark. The good news for industry is that younger workers coming into the workforce are becoming more data literate with each graduating class. Over time and with the right hiring practices, your company can begin to exploit your own data using your own, data-savvy employees just as Lufthansa has done.

While the Lufthansa story is a great success story, it is only a first step in a journey to data analytics maturity. The solution described in this story is an example of a predictive model. As Lufthansa has shown, predictive models are clearly useful. However, my recommendation for the next step in extracting data value is to explore the creation of prescriptive models. Is there more value in predicting a flight will be late, or in prescribing an action to ensure it arrives on-time? Prescriptive analytics is an emerging area of data analytics. It often is an ensemble of several data science technologies such a neural network, graph database/analytics, and simulation.

One last observation about this story. Industry experience is showing the effectiveness of an organization's data analytics (data science) initiative is often directly related to the maturity of its data governance program. There is a symbiotic relationship emerging *between these seemingly disparate programs. The first step in data analytics is knowing what data are available in the organization to analyze. This is exactly the goal of data governance, understanding what data the organization has, what is in it, and where is it is located. Data acquisition standards can also expedite the procurement of external data often needed to augment data analytics models. Although data analytics is often quite experimental in nature, it still needs controls. When new models are validated and staged for production, they first need to conform to standards for explainability, transparency, training bias, risk, and ethics. Conversely, machine learning, natural language processing, and other data science technologies are beginning to make strides in automating many aspects of data governance such as building and updating data catalogs, processes usually performed manually by data stewards. Fostering the relationship between data analytics and data governance could be part of a winning strategy for your organization.*

88: Computer-Based Simulation for Real Savings

#usa #northamerica #healthcare #medical #personalcare #hygiene
#crm #modeling #simulation #analytics #predictive #product #cpg

The Procter & Gamble Company (P&G) is an American multinational consumer goods corporation specializing in a wide range of personal/consumer health, personal care, and hygiene products with almost 5 billion consumers throughout18 countries.

The conglomerate produces 50 leading brands, 25 of them billion-dollar brands. P&G products cover over 1,500 different websites, attracting 1 billion visitors. They have 500 different CRM programs touching over 100 million consumers. They send 1.2 billion emails per year.

P&G has recognized the potential of Big Data and has put a strong emphasis on using it to make better, smarter, real-time business decisions in business units around the globe. The Global Business Services organization has developed tools, systems, and processes to provide managers with direct access to the latest data and advanced analytics.

P&G has extensively used computer-based simulation analytics to design and evaluate virtual replicas prior to their manufacture. Instead of hand-crafting a new design for a disposable diaper, P&G uses modeling and simulation to create thousands of iterations. In seconds, they are able to find the best design for a disposable diaper. They move to the real-world prototype phase only when the virtual replicas satisfy their quality parameters.

In the case of developing a new dishwashing liquid, P&G used predictive analytics and simulation models to predict how moisture would excite various fragrance molecules, so consumers get the right fragrance notes at the right time throughout the dishwashing process.

Simulation analytics helps to ensure optimal product performance by taking into account many different variables and creating and altering different models or designs virtually.

With predictive analytics and simulation, thousands of design person-hours are saved. The shortest time-to-market, or the time to put the product into the commercial phase is achieved.

Expert Analysis by Barr Moses,

Co-founder and CEO, Monte Carlo

Immediately, I was drawn to one phrase in this case study: "shortest time-to-market." At Monte Carlo, I often use the phrase "measure in minutes," in other words, be mindful of how you spend your time — it can make all the difference. For nearly any company, determining where (and how) to allocate your time is one of the most important differentiators when it comes to staying ahead of the competition. Not surprisingly, then, simulation analytics is a valuable tool for any organization looking to "measure in minutes" by reducing time-to-market for their products.

It's also worth noting that in P&G's case, modeling alone doesn't design a perfect diaper. Rather, it helps P&G reach the prototype stage incredibly fast—at which point, presumably, talented disposable-diaper engineers take over to turn the prototype into the ideal final product. That's a lesson many executives could stand to learn: Analytics, and even machine learning, rarely replaces human ingenuity, but it can help save enormous amounts of time and manual labor along the way. And those saved resources often mean your analytics program pays for itself.

89: Fixing False Fraud Flags Finds Favor with Financial Customers

#usa #northamerica #financial #banking #loans #fraud
#cloud #automation #customer #document

There are situations that people could never really prepare for—from car accidents to medical emergencies. Among the things that people worry about the most are the expenses they will incur because of those incidents. That's where Axcess Financial comes in. For 25 years, the company and its affiliates have helped various people from different backgrounds get the money they need through loans and other services.

Although most people who request loans have good and honest intentions, they cannot be said for all applicants. As the business steadily grew, so did the number of fraudulent applications, which soon led to substantial monetary loss. Axcess Financial now needed to find a solution to find and conform to modern identity fraud trends as soon as possible.

One challenge that the company faced was that once criminals discover the new system, they can easily exploit it. Many experienced criminals can easily reverse-engineer various systems. The company needed a new system that's reliable and not easily hacked by criminals.

After evaluating various fraud technology vendors, they ultimately chose SAS Identity 360. This system is a cloud-based software that enables groups to gather different authentication data providers for a fast and centralized authentication of online users. By collecting data from different sources using analytics from SAS, Axcess Financial can easily detect fraudsters. As a result, just within months, the number of losses dropped dramatically.

According to Richard Cooney, Axcess Financial's Fraud Director, the company managed to identify and deal with at least 70% of their fraud problem. They've resolved various first-party fraud and even virtually eliminated 80% of third-party frauds. Not only has the system quickly identified fraud but it also removed various time-consuming procedures. Now, internal agents can resolve and identify fraud claims within five minutes. This procedure used to take several hours before it could be resolved. As the minute the SAS system went live, hackers or fraudsters were unable to attack, with their hit rate lowering to 0%.

Furthermore, Axcess Financial also lessened the remaining conflicts in the application process. Before the implementation of the current fraud system, several good clients were inconvenienced with the slow application and authentication process, as well as false positives. With the current system, the company now enables legitimate clients to easily glide through the entire application process. With the amount of dropped false positives, 10% of loan seekers don't even need to authenticate anymore.

Expert Analysis by Althea Davis

Managing Partner and Chief Data Officer at Avantologie | 2021 Global Data Power Women | Board Member (IsCDO.org) | Ambassador to the UAE for IsCDO.org | CDO Magazine Editorial Board Member

Axcess Financial apparently operated on antiquated systems to miss a looming giant of collective bad actors to create significant monetary losses. It would suggest that the system had gapping wounds that primarily internal bad actors take advantage and mostly like sold and or cooperated in the fraud as reverse engineering and re-producing data has a high probability of internal execution and/or cooperation.

Bad actors had Axcess wrapped up in circles; an unusually high level of re-work which resulted in neglect and unnecessary high friction customer experience.

With its newfound freedom to connect to the customer from onboarding, relationship building and engaging, Axcess galvinize its journey with rich linked contextualize data to better interact and meet the needs of its customers in a frictionless matter to create those wow moments. Stepping the data sophistication with knowledge graphs and data talent beyond the usual suspects; data scientist to fuel the data gems knowledge engineers, data curators, ontologist and behavioural psychologist for example. Axcess will create exponential growth and diversify its portfolio to make better use of the trust establish when clients are in a difficult situation. These same customers may be more likely to access financial knowledge sharing in good times and/ or make better use of curated data to help manage other customers in is customer servicing role.

90: FASTER CHURN AND CROSS-SELLING PREVENTS ANALYTICS HANG-UPS

#telco #austria #europe #customer #churn
#visualization #predictive #marketing #sales

T-*Mobile Austria is a subsidiary* of T-Mobile International, a holding company for Deutsche Telekom's mobile communications subsidiaries, which owns it.

The acquisition of Tele.Ring by T-Mobile International effectively increased the number of customers of T Mobile Austria y 50%. With a new customer base of 3.2 million, their market share increased significantly against the market leader, Mobilkom Austria. They developed a post-acquisition strategy to increase average revenue per customer, decrease customer churn, and address the saturated market and price erosion. Data mining was seen as critical to their continued success.

Since 1999, T-Mobile Austria had been running data mining models for churn and cross-selling that had become outdated and cumbersome to maintain and operate. A new software solution, Portrait Miner from Pitney Bowes, proved to be significantly easier to implement, better performing, and more cost-effective to license.

Using the data build utility and automated deployment functionality, multiple predictive models, especially for upsell and cross-sell, could now be created more easily. The speed and 3D visualization capabilities of the software made possible the close real-time cooperation between analysts and segment managers. Faster business decisions and more streamlined operations stemmed from the availability of the Portrait Miner for use by technical department, marketing, and sales. In particular, more diverse predictive modeling applications could be used to determine retention optimization for contract subscribers, help prevent inactivity for prepay subscribers, and optimize network rollout.

The Portrait solution also enabled the T-Mobile campaign management team to become more effective in executing complex selections and accurately targeting the right customers, with the right offer, at the right time.

Portrait Miner, which is now actively used within T-Mobile Austria has improved response times for analytical requests and freed up power analysts to add real value to the business as opposed to simply managing queries and reports. Using rapid predictive tools, the marketing team now is able to create highly targeted campaigns and render faster and better decisions.

T-Mobile Austria achieved a 20% reduction in churn along with a significant decrease in software costs estimated at several hundred thousand Euros along with savings of tens of thousands of Euros per year on staffing the solution.

Expert Analysis by Paul Schindler

Founder and CEO, Schindler Technology

The key points of the story are:

- *Automated analytics and visualizations*

- *Predictive/what if modeling*

A common pain point for organizations is the level of effort and time involved to produce analytics and visualizations. Too often his requires cumbersome consolidating of data from legacy sources and exhaustive spreadsheet work. This creates delays in getting the information to those that need it, and bogs down organization employees that could otherwise be spending time on other tasks.

Automating the analytics only gets organizations part way. Unfortunately, too many organizations stop the automation there. It's the predictive modeling component that provides the critical link of turning the analytics into actionable and timely business decisions.

At T-Mobile Austria, the tool is being used by the technical department, marketing, and sales. They should expand the use to other parts of the company. Organizations have benefited by also utilizing this functionally in other areas, such as for decisions regarding compensation planning, recruitment, succession planning, span of control, org shape, and diversity.

91: Driving High-Speed Innovation and Fan Engagement

#usa #northamerica #europe #automobile #racing
#sports #competition #streaming #media #entertainment
#monitoring #automation #predictive #customer

The National Association for Stock Car Auto Racing (NASCAR) is an American auto racing sanctioning and operating company. Best known for stock-car racing, it was founded in 1948. It is headquartered in Daytona Beach, Florida. NASCAR sanctions over 1,500 races at over 100 tracks in 48 US states as well as in Canada, Mexico, and Europe every year. NASCAR races are broadcast in 150 countries. It is the second-most-watched sport on TV after the NFL.

Car racing is fiercely competing for sports fans with more modern sports and international competitions being held to woo sports fans. Additionally, sports enthusiasts have multiple options to follow their favorite sports, which include network broadcasts, cable channels, or stream events to their smartphones, PCs, or tablets.

NASCAR wanted to leverage both social and traditional media to engage more effectively with racing fans and create better entertainment experience while providing business intelligence to the NASCAR ecosystem.

As a result, NASCAR established the Fan and Media Engagement Center (FMEC). Created in a partnership with Hewlett-Packard (HP) Enterprise Services, the center is designed to help NASCAR and its partners improve the NASCAR fan experience based on insights from a variety of media, including social, digital, television, video, print, and radio.

To assist with the monitoring of all and anything being talked or written about on broadcasts, blogging, television, video, and traditional media that has to do with the NASCAR brand, HP employed several automated, embedded management and monitoring tools, and built-in redundancy, to ensure the FMEC would meet NASCAR's requirements for around-the-clock availability. HP implemented its Vertica Data Analytics Platform, a columnar database that supports high-speed data queries. A highly scalable platform, it uses probabilistic and pattern-matching algorithms to recognize concepts and relationships in both structured and unstructured data. HP then installed a powerful software from its Big Data Analytics—HPE IDOL (Intelligent Data Operating Layer) to address NASCAR's fundamental business challenge—the need to extract actionable insights hidden within terabytes of data.

Analyzing the data enables NASCAR to assess fans' responses to events and drivers. Actionable data helps NASCAR make more effective decisions about investments and corporate direction.

The technology brought a lot of benefits for NASCAR. It helped create positive buzz to keep NASCAR top-of-mind, keep fans engaged, and reinforce the strength of the NASCAR brand. The volumes of NASCAR-related social mentions rose 55% across national races. All these contribute to help NASCAR compete more effectively for sports fans, which translates into higher ticket sales.

It likewise delivers more value to sponsors and partners through its data collection, analysis, and reporting capabilities to produce a brand analysis that enables the sponsor to devise more effective and impactful social media campaigns. Its ability to validate the impact of NASCAR events help win sponsorship for them, helping to offset the overhead costs of events and improving NASCAR's profitability. Another important benefit is the ability of the company to now be more proactive in its public relations considering media coverage and public sentiment.

Expert Analysis by Ido Biger

VP Technology, Chief information and Data Officer, EL AL Israel Airlines

NASCAR have utilized the ever-growing data feeds and decided to be a major player in the game of the data driven companies that derives operational acts based on generated insights.

The most interesting technological part that is missing in the paragraph is the architecture and the data processing both on the engineering part (structure the unstructured) and the analytical phase (which techniques were used to drive those insights that generated the mentions by 55% for example).

Such project usually starts with the business goal which later drives the needs and sources relevant for the solution—in this case—mostly social media. Gathering social media in real time (the data velocity isn't mentioned) will require several tools/methods that are not mentioned here as well.

Still, it sounds as a great example of a traditional industry adopting of the possibilities hidden in the big data and analytics world. With regards to the data / insights shared with the sponsors, it would be interesting to hear and understand more.

92: SMOKING-OUT COMMUNITY FIRE RISKS

#netherlands #europe #firesafety #firedepartment #emergencyservices
#government #datawarehouse #predictive #monitoring #image #map

The *Amsterdam Fire Department* provides fire safety services to the residents of the city of Amsterdam in the Netherlands including fire suppression, emergency medical services/ ambulance transport, advanced life support, fire investigation, enforcement of NYS Fire Prevention & Building Codes, and public education.

The Fire Department believes that to create smarter emergency services, harnessing data is the key. An app that simply contains growing information created and collected is no longer sufficient. Access to the data is what is needed; data transfer must be two-way. So, the Amsterdam Fire Department publishes its data in an open format. It published 'Firebrary', a library of technical terms developed so that everyone can have a common understanding. They likewise post live tweets of fire incidents that contain links to detailed data of the event where firefighters could know the full details of the incident in seconds and could be forewarned.

The department also mapped the environment in which the emergency services operate using Big Data. With the business intelligence software called QlikView, implemented by QlikTech's Dutch partner Incentro, information from the data warehouse is processed, analyzed, and displayed on a map. This involved using data of past fires to map high-risk areas and other metrics such as the economic background to develop insights on these patterns. These insights can help with deciding where stations should be located and measuring personnel performance.

They produced a completely new kind of risk profile—the first for the Netherlands. It calculated the risk of all the buildings, roads, waterways, and train rails in the region—involving 600,000 objects!

This has enabled the service to pinpoint 12 million possible incidents. Where there is a particular risk, they can have the right resources and equipment in place. Training for staff is tailored accordingly and households in identified risk areas can get fire safety advice.

Over 50 fire services worldwide are now using this system; they are part of 1,500 public sector organizations in total that rely on its effective benefits.

Expert Analysis by Theresa Kushner

Consultant, AI/Analytics at NTT DATA

Collaboration—it is the new dynamic that is making data much more available and, in turn, more valuable. Amsterdam Fire Department shows the world how collaborating with data suppliers, their own internal operations, and even tool providers, such as QlikView, can help expand service offerings to their communities. What they found was that sharing data in an open, understandable format gives them access to additional data that helps them map services and predict risk more effectively.

Governmental organizations are not usually the first thought of when considering innovation with Big Data. However, the Amsterdam Fire Department has done that by putting their data to work in such unique ways that it has created a new kind of risk profile for the Netherlands that helps pinpoint millions of possible incidents. This feat is even more impressive when considering that it was accomplished against the backdrop of European data sharing regulations. What the Amsterdam Fire Department has proven is that data—when properly managed and used to create value — is always in high demand.

93: Putting a Premium on Predictive Analytics

#belgium #france #europe #insurance #marketing
#predictive #segmentation #behavior #customer

Founded in 1931, *Corona Direct* is the first direct insurer in Belgium and the country's second-largest direct insurance company. It is a subsidiary of the Belgian-French banking and insurance company DEXIA.

As a direct insurance company, Corona Direct works from one central office and doesn't partner with intermediaries. This enables them to save on unnecessary costs and offer cheaper insurance premiums for a wide range of products, including car, fire, and property insurance. The company promotes its products to prospects and potential clients through four primary channels, including direct marketing, website, call center, and affinity insurance writing in which the company underwrites insurance programs for third-party vendors.

While the company's growth was rapidly accelerating through direct marketing and customer acquisition campaigns, revenues from newly acquired insurance policies were not profitable and did not generate returns. The plan was to use the first-year revenues generated from new insurance policies to pay for the expenses incurred by the acquisition campaigns. However, what happened was the total cost of acquiring new clients is almost 50% more than the first-year revenues. Corona Direct could not continue this trend as this would put the company's growth strategy at risk.

Corona Direct decided to implement IBM SPSS predictive analytics software to make its marketing strategies into profitable campaigns. The software helped the company's marketing team to efficiently create, develop, and execute optimized and well-targeted outbound marketing campaigns. The predictive analysis feature of the tool enables the company to identify audience segments that are highly likely to respond to a campaign. Once identified, they will then send targeted sales ads to them.

"We were mailing four million letters annually at an average cost of $.50 per letter. We decided on a strategy that would help us mail less while maintaining our prospect conversion rate, so we looked for software that would enable us to achieve this goal. After modeling using IBM SPSS software and then fine-tuning our prospect mailings, we were able to reduce our costs by 30% while maintaining new customer conversion rates," Philippe Neyt, Commercial Director of Corona Direct, shared.

Predictive analytics, user behavior identification, and segmentation all helped the company perform a smart profit-cost analysis, balancing growth targets against profit margins. As a result, Corona Direct is now able to optimize its marketing strategies and further boost its growth potential.

With this solution, the company's campaign costs were reduced by 30%, customer profitability increased by 20%, and ROI was achieved within 6 months.

94: Cutting-Out Surgical Supply Waste and Inefficiencies

#usa #northamerica #hospital #medical #healthcare #patient
#monitoring #analytics #modeling #finance #supplier

Founded in 1953, Memorial Healthcare System (MHS) is a healthcare facility located in South Florida. It is one of the largest public healthcare providers in the country and highly recognized for its quality healthcare services, superior patient—and family-centered care, and high employee satisfaction rating.

Many hospitals fail to closely track of all the equipment and supplies they use for surgery. Often, they monitor only about 20% of their surgical tools for cost efficiency and availability. MHS, however, wanted to continuously optimize their processes, reduce costs, and provide improved patient care services at affordable fees by closely monitoring the efficiency of their operating rooms and availability of all their surgical supplies, including medical and surgical supplies, including gloves, sutures, sponges, and other surgical devices. Additionally, they wanted to check and control each item as used by which doctor for which patient and for what type of surgery, to aid in improving surgical outcomes.

To do this, MHS deployed Pyramid Analytics' BI Office, an enterprise business intelligence and analytics platform that enables and empowers users to model and analyze their data using a single BI solution, on top of the hospital's Microsoft SQL Server. The combination of BI Office and SQL server enabled MHS to analyze up to 500GB of data from multiple sources.

The powerful system helped the hospital's staff in the finance department to compare prices of surgical supplies and equipment from different manufacturers and quickly decide if switching to another vendor can reduce cost without compromising quality. Moreover, it also helped clinical staff to easily identify in demand procedures, measure the time each surgeon takes in performing a particular operation, and analyze demographic data to determine population segments that require specific surgical needs.

These pieces of information contributed to the operating room efficiencies, supply cost reduction, and improved patient care. By using an advanced and powerful BI and analytics platform, MHS is able to track the usage of 100% of its surgical devices based on type of surgery, doctor, and patient, and optimize ROI by maximizing efficiency, cutting costs, and improving outcomes.

Expert Analysis by Scott Taylor

The Data Whisperer & Principal Consultant at MetaMeta Consulting

The health of an enterprise like MHS, depends on the health of their critical data elements. Not only did MHS achieve impressive results from their investments in BI and analytics platforms, but they also implemented strategic data management steps early in their journey. MHS standardized and mastered their disparate data about medical supplies, doctors, patients and types of surgeries. Absent this foundational data, the analytics could never provide these powerful insights into opportunities for operational efficiency, maximizing vendor relationships and most importantly improving care for their patients.

MHS clearly has a strong data governance and stewardship team that was able to articulate the value of their work to leadership. Going forward, MHS should continue its enterprise data governance program and perhaps highlight further the contributions that the data management team makes to the overall analytical success. They are a shining example of a best practice for data standards. Master data isn't the sexy stuff, but without it these deeper benefits are simply not possible at scale.

95: CONSTRUCTING A SMART SOLUTION TO REAL ESTATE SITE PLANNING

#UK #europe #property #realestate #housing #datascience
#cloud #customer #location #visualization #recommendation

Jones Lang LaSalle. Inc. (JLL) has been London's property market leader for more than 200 years, specializing in commercial property and investment management. JLL works with real estate owners, occupiers, and investors worldwide by providing property advice and real estate services to help them succeed in one of today's most in-demand business sectors.

Due to sudden changes in the demographic, economic, and technological landscape across the city of London, a new market for commercial real estate in the city opened, and JLL needed a modern site planning tool to attract international business clients and convince them of the advantages of working and expanding their operations in this new, emerging market. The company wanted to give potential commercial real estate clients a good head start in moving, relocating, and bringing their business operations in London. To do this, they needed a solution that can process huge amounts of data and convert them into accurate, insightful, and up-to-date information that clients can access and use through a centralized platform and without the need for GIS) knowledge.

JLL implemented cloud computing, GIS), web-mapping, and spatial data science tools, to build a location intelligence application called GROW.London. This is a web application that equips clients with relevant data and valuable insights to help them make sound decisions about business location and expansion based on various factors, including connectivity, competitiveness, markets, living, and talent. Presented in charts, graphs, and interactive maps, the application displays useful data such as population increases, existing and emerging key office markets, economic growth, employment statistics, residential housing prices, and transportation network improvements — all of which helpful to commercial real estate clients as they decide to invest in London business hub.

Using 10 years of historical data, GROW.London can present accurate data with a better sense of price increases and market fluctuations. This feature helps calculate market competitiveness, housing price changes, and employment and economic growth. These insights enable JLL to accelerate the site planning process for clients and increase investment opportunities throughout the city.

Expert Analysis by Chris Geissler

CEO and Co-Founder, Asgard Data, and Professor at
Lake Forest Graduate School of Management

The JLL case reminds me of what Zillow does by using public records and other open data to offer a differentiated service. While it seems like a marketing strategy, JLL created a new product to address common questions. Products such as these change customer conversations and expectations.

GROW.London educates clients and uplevels conversations through simplifying factors to consider when locating business operations in London. Further, there are no barriers such as a paywall or sign-up process to access these insights. JLL uses information as a brand differentiator and empowers clients. Insight-leading companies are known for offering summarized, data-supported, market observations. Consider how often McKinsey or Gartner analysts are quoted when justifying a business case.

However, data products are a long-term commitment and cool website widgets become customer expectations. Therefore, JLL must treat GROW.London as a legitimate product with appropriate product management and support. LinkedIn and Google are infamous for creating experimental tools and products then turn them off and disappoint customers.

96: DEMAND GENERATION DEMANDS ADVANCED ANALYTICS

#usa #northamerica #marketing #customer #sales #crm
#seo #customer #predictive #monitoring #modeling

Founded in 1986, *Trident Marketing* is a multi-channel direct response marketing company based in North Carolina that specializes in marketing, sales, lead generation, and customer acquisition for leading US consumer brands. The company handles over 4M calls annually for its clients.

While Trident Marketing runs targeted marketing campaigns for its clients to acquire paying customers at minimum sales costs, it lacked relevant data and key insights about the performance and effectiveness of all its campaigns across different channels. The company didn't have the tools and ability to measure simple conversion rates or analyze why some sales pitches worked while others didn't. To run highly-targeted, successful demand-generation marketing campaigns, the company needed to gain better visibility of its campaigns across channels and insightful analysis of each campaign's performance.

To address these challenges, Trident Marketing deployed IBM's PureData System for Analytics, a simple data appliance designed to capture, optimize, and analyze massive amounts of data in a fast and streamlined process. With this tool, Trident Marketing captured huge volumes of data from multiple sources and channels, including their call center, CRM application, order systems, search engines, and credit bureaus to understand customers' behavior and predict how they would respond to campaigns across different platforms.

Now with relevant data available on hand and the ability to turn these data into key insights, the company can quickly identify the right time to call a customer, which specific product to promote, and which salesperson is ideally the best to close the sale. Additionally, using sophisticated analytic models, they can now predict which customers have the tendency to cancel their client's services within 12 months. Finally, the analysis of click-stream data acquired from organic searches helps the company identify the right keywords to bid on and optimize its PPC campaigns.

With Trident Marketing's sales and marketing campaigns being more targeted, optimized, and effective, the company's revenue skyrocketed by 1000% in four consecutive years, while sales increased by 10% in the first 60 days of implementing the solution. The company also improved its pay-per-click (PPC) bids, click-through and conversion rates, cost per call and close rates, and other key metrics.

Expert Analysis by Keyur Desai
EVP of Enterprise Data & Analytics, Herbalife

The first item that jumps out is the outsized Revenue growth Trident Marketing experienced after becoming data driven. Data and Analytics has always had the ability to generate outsized

Business Outcomes, and a 1000% increase in only 4 years puts it among the fastest growing companies, globally. This is what data can do, and if more evidence is needed, we just have to look at Amazon, Google and Facebook and yet other examples. Also notice how quickly Trident Marketing began to see the benefits of a data driven approach. Within 60 days they saw a 10% revenue increase. A healthy increase, quickly!

To gain this impact Trident Marketing did not just put all data into the IBM Puredata System and see immediate value. It took time, and there were multiple dimensions of work here. 1. Trident Marketing had to ensure they could uniquely identify a Person no matter the channel. This is where Master Data Management capabilities had to have been implemented and creating this "Person Master" is a key component of an analytical system that allows us to better understand Customer behavior. 2. Trident Marketing also had to ensure it was able to adequately comply with CCPA, GDPR and other Data Specific Regulations as much of the data they collect is considered Personally Identifiable Information. They must have had to do this by ensuring they had a Data Governance and Data Quality program in place. 3. Trident Marketing also had to have created a Data Fluency effort to ensure its own employees understood how to use, work with and communicate using data and analytics.

Opportunities Trident Marketing may choose to explore in the future are: 1. Improve its Operating Leverage by using data, analytics and artificial intelligence to enable as many prospects/customers to self-serve through a call center call as successfully as they would have if they had spoken with a live person. This capability utilizes data and analytics to hyper personalize the call center or chat experience and transform it into a human-like chatbot experience, greatly reducing expense growth. 2. Use the data they collect to create a new revenue contributor for their company: A Data Business. Other corporations *would be interested in knowing about consumer trends overall and by specific geographic areas. Trident Marketing is at the center of acquiring much of the data needed to provide these insights. It will be important for Trident Marketing to ensure this data has been aggregated enough to de-identify a specific Prospect/Customer.*

97: Claiming Success over Insurance Fraud

#global #germany #europe #insurance #fraud
#diagnostic #automation #monitoring #customer

In the world of insurance, vehicle-related fraud is the most common insurance fraud. This includes fake or manipulated car accidents and hugely exaggerated damage claims. However, homeowners or owners of immovable properties are testing the insurance agency's internal audit mechanisms. Several insurance agencies have been a victim of these frauds, one of them being Allianz Insurance.

As fraud grew rampant, agencies now needed not only a fast solution but a reliable and long-lasting one. According to Maya Mašková, Internal Audit Department Head of Allianz Insurance, the insurance agency needed to replace its outdated fraud-detection system. They needed to be assured that it would find suspicious behavior ordinary people would not notice.

To resolve this problem, Allianz Insurance used the SAS Detection and Investigation for insurance. This system uses a hybrid approach when sifting through data. This involves several statistical techniques

301

to look at data from different angles. This helps companies uncover things that a person cannot easily see.

By using a hybrid or mixed approach, it lets companies save in claim compensations. It notably increased the number of identified fraud cases and even helped improve the company's operating procedures.

This solution enables suspicious behavior to be automatically identified and easily presented to investigators every single day. Investigators now can focus on cases with a high potential in financial damage or a high probability of fraud.

Additionally, it also helps company investigators reveal social networks, particularly beneficial in revealing organized fraud. It helps investigators connect all the entities related to the case, as the system gives a detailed image of all the links. This would also help hasten the case without needing to do the usual routine examination procedures. Due to this, several organized fraud units now refrain from targeting Allianz Insurance.

Since the company implemented this solution they have expanded the amount and type of insurance more than they usually examine. Now users can browse through the monitored elements, which would give the company a real boost in efficiency and savings. This even led to the discovery of several major fraud organizations.

During the first six months, Allianz insurance, they were able to identify more than a thousand insurance fraud cases that were worth more than $62 million. The number of identified fraud cases increased significantly, with 426 fraud cases more than in the same period just a year before.

Expert Analysis by Penny Wand

Senior Partner, Technology Practice, Data
Engineering and Analytics, West Monroe

The interesting point here is the integration of human and AI interaction within a critical business function, which provides better visibility to the investigator to aid decision-making. Further, this example creates a virtuous cycle. Solving for efficiency AND fraud simultaneously ultimately impacts premiums charged and drives even more profitability for the company top and bottom line. I particularly appreciate how just this capability has discouraged other bad actors from targeting Allianz, further improving Allianz results.

Going forward, this company might consider integrating pictures and voice analysis to improve the claim-handling process and potentially identifying fraud in this manner and enable better claim estimation. This could be extended with auto shops to improve estimating and repair costs and facilitation of improved quotes.

98: DIALING UP CUSTOMER RETENTION

#pakistan #asia #telecom #communication #datamining
#automation #predictive #analytics #customer #marketing

Headquartered in Islamabad, Jazz (rebranded from Mobilink in 2017) is Pakistan's first mobile communications service provider that offers a range of postpaid and prepaid SMS, voice, and data telecommunication services to corporate and individual subscribers. Currently owned by the Russian operator Vimpelcom (now VEON Ltd.), Jazz has a subscriber base of over 50 million.

Because more than 99% of the telecom's subscribers are prepaid users with no contract commitment, it was difficult for Jazz to manage these users, build customer trust, and decrease churn. There was no way of engaging with them on a more targeted and personal level, which often led to customer inactivity, loss, and churn.

Jazz partnered with KXEN, a data mining automation company, now part of SAP, that offers predictive analytics and business intelligence, and deployed its flagship product called the InfiniteInsight. The tool is designed to optimize each step in the customer lifecycle

304

— from acquisition to cross-sell and up-sell to retention and next best activity. Jazz leveraged InfiniteInsight to easily identify potential churners even before they opt out of the service and to implement a "next best activity" architecture through intelligent predictive models and strategic segmentation.

To gain a better understanding of the behaviors of its prepaid customers and the complex nature of its retail network, Jazz used InfiniteInsight combined with clustering techniques and was able to discover insights such as 32% of retailers have a very loyal customer base and 25% of subscribers recharge from their preferred retailer. With this information, the company was able to create more effective advertisements targeted to specific outlets and provide incentives to retailers that can acquire, boost, and retain specific segments of Jazz's subscriber base.

InfiniteInsight gave Jazz the ability to analyze massive amounts of data, including millions of subscribers' data and billions of call records, and acquire insights that helped them improve efficiency, boost loyalty, and save costs. By accurately targeting customers, the uptake of customer retention offers increased 8-fold from 0.5% to 4% while spending a fraction of the cost. Campaign response rates also improved by 380%.

"InfiniteInsight lets us analyze thousands of customer attributes for predictive power. It's a paradigm shift to the way that we think about the return on big data and we look forward to exploring new big data sources to build on this success," Mirza Yousaf, Assistant Manager of Advanced Analytics at Jazz, shared.

Expert Analysis by Neil Jain

Partner, Software & High-Tech, Private Equity, SaaS
Transformation and Customer Success, West Monroe

Given the huge investments mobile operators make in infrastructure, sustaining and growing revenue that takes advantage of that network is critical to their profitability. Jazz provides a great example of leveraging a combination of data sources (retail distribution, customer data, usage / transaction records, billing data, etc.) to drive key profit levers like reducing customer acquisition cost (CAC) and growing average revenue per user (ARPU).

Generating this kind of insight is especially complex in these environments for two reasons. The first complexity is the sheer data volume (e.g., 50M+ subscribers with hundreds of transactions per day) and velocity (constant evolution of data as subscribers join / leave and more calls / texts / purchases are made). The second complexity is that this data often sits across multiple, often antiquated, systems (e.g., operations systems, billing systems, customer databases, retail transaction systems, etc.).

Going forward, it would be interesting to see how these data-driven insights could be leveraged across different customer touchpoints. One could imagine leveraging alerts and/or next-best-action recommendations through multiple channels—pushed to the mobile phone, Jazz customer web portal, as a pop-up for customer support agents, included on the monthly billing statement, etc.

99: Cashing-In on Preventing Cash-Outs

#singapore #asia #banking #financial #insurance #investment
#transaction #predictive #customer #analytics #prescriptive

What's worse than not finding an ATM when you badly need cash? Finding one that doesn't dispense any because it ran out of cash! Don't you find this annoying? For DBS, they know that this situation causes a major inconvenience to customers, which is why they stepped up and did something to prevent this scenario.

DBS Bank Ltd, based in Singapore, is a multinational banking and financial services group with presence across Asia. DBS offers a wide selection of personal banking and financial planning products, including savings and deposits, insurance, personal loans, investments, refinancing, and online banking services.

With a network of more than 1,100 ATMs in Singapore, DBS processes over 25 million transactions monthly, making it one of the busiest in the world. This means a downtime or an out-of-cash scenario in just one ATM can spell trouble for customers.

To prevent this and ensure that its machines are operating optimally and effectively at all times, DBS needed a solution that could intelligently analyze withdrawal data in their ATMs to predict customer behavior, minimize out-of-cash occurrences, and make better decisions. The bank partnered with SAS Analytics to build and launch an innovative solution that analyzes customers' withdrawal data from each ATM, predicts upcoming activities, and optimizes the cash loading process.

By using the SAS Forecast Server software, DBS can convert these data into an execution plan that enables them to reload cash in machines at the right time, minimizing undesirable situations, such as downtimes and running out of cash. This intelligent solution also enables DBS to cater to unique and special withdrawal patterns, such as during festivities, peak travel seasons, as well as pay periods during the end of the month.

As a result, DBS was able to reduce ATM out-of-cash scenarios by 90%. A total of 30,000 hours of customer wait time have also been eliminated, while the number of customers affected by the cash reloading process was down by 350,000 compared to the previous year. Finally, the number of trips in reloading ATMs was reduced by 10%, while returning amount of leftover cash from the machines to the bank has decreased by 30%

With the successful execution of this innovative and proprietary solution, DBS was awarded top honors in the Singapore Government's National Infocomm Awards for the Most Innovative Use of Infocomm Technology (Private Sector—General). Considered the first-of-its-kind in the banking industry in Singapore, this strategy helped improve the efficiency of DBS' ATM Network, as well as customer satisfaction.

Expert Analysis by David Steier

Distinguished Service Professor of Data Science
and AI at Carnegie Mellon University

Kudos are due to DBS both for using sophisticated analytics to address this challenge, and tracking business outcomes so closely. The prediction of the amount of cash needed by an ATM, like many real-world forecasting problems, is difficult because of the number of factors and nature of constraints involved. A simple time-series forecast based on historical data might capture some of the simple patterns that repeat regularly, such as dependency on day of week, but it would miss more complex factors such as occasional special events that might increase demands for cash.

The solution needs to minimize a variety of outcomes from poor predictions (out-of-cash, idle cash, extra trips to reload cash, and downtime that makes customers wait) argues for a multi-objective optimization approach, while the presence of domain knowledge and customer preferences (running out of notes of a certain denomination is bad, but not as bad as completely running out of cash) means artificial intelligence techniques will apply.

Data integration (of historical data, real-time cash levels at each ATM, special circumstances, etc.) is a challenge with these types of data-driven models, as is regularly updating the prediction model as customer behavior changes over time, for example due to a generally decreasing use of cash.

For the future, one possibility worth investigating is whether cash levels at nearby ATMs are correlated with each other and might be used to optimize reloading trips or even providing early warnings of potential out-of-cash ATMs located one that is running low.

100: PUTTING A STOP TO FREQUENT HIGHWAY STOPPING

#usa #northamerica #metrotech #intellisection #traffic #sensor
#realtimedata #automation #monitoring #prescriptive #video

Santa Clara County, also known as the "Silicon Valley," is the 7th largest county in California with a population of about 2 million. Silicon Valley is a highly urbanized county. As a consequence, traffic congestion continues to be a primary concern among commuters around the area. The time lost in traffic translates to reduced quality of life and lower business productivity, negatively impacting the economy.

To help address the problem, Santa Clara County deployed MetroTech's IntelliSection technology on 107 intersections in 2012, including its five busiest expressways. This traffic analysis software of MetroTech leverages video feeds from roadside cameras installed on existing infrastructures to aid transportation management systems, connected vehicles, and mobile applications by providing them with accurate and real-time traffic flow data.

This software helps mitigate congestion by utilizing the traffic data it gathers to synchronize signals across intersections, ramps, arterials, and freeways. It monitors lane-level vehicle counts, headway, and speed then sends these data to Traffic Control Centers (TCC) in real-time. Additionally, it is capable of generating automated "push-to-screen" accident notifications for TCCs, reducing the need to constantly focus on the screen while increasing the detection of new events.

A year after the deployment of this technology in Santa Clara County, a case study was conducted to analyze its efficiency in the area. Data were taken from seventeen intersections encompassing the Lawrence Expressway, one of the county's busiest expressways with about 600,000 daily commuters. The analysis showed a 3% decrease in stops, which equates to around 18,000 fewer daily vehicle stops.

The sample data from the Lawrence Expressway was then used to project the benefits of IntelliSection deployed on 107 intersections across the County. For the first year, the estimated travel time savings were 805,500 hours; fuel consumption savings were 984,300 gallons; NOx emission reduction was by 14.71 tons; CO emission reduction was by 75.52 tons, and VOC emission reduction was by 17.5 tons.

Expert Analysis by Douglas Laney
Data & Analytics Innovation Fellow, West Monroe

It's hardly a surprise that a city in California would lead the way in creatively reducing commuter frustration and automobile emissions, and less of a surprise that the city at the heart of Silicon Valley would apply intelligent sensors and AI to do so. Moreover, in today's digital economy, I expect to see more businesses like MetroTech emerge to digitize dumb processes in every industry. But also notice the triple-play value proposition: individuals win, the city wins, and the environment wins. Can your analytics do this, or are you still stuck creating more and more hindsight-oriented dashboards?

What process today cannot incorporate sensors and intelligence to be optimized? Not many at all. Yet, how many of these processes have yet to be digitized and productized? Most. Cars that drive themselves on roads that self-manage the traffic, is a metaphor for and a bellwether of the business of tomorrow, or what we call "the self-driving organization." The speed of business today already has proven to be operationally too fast for the human brain. And with sufficient computing power and data inputs—not just from within the organization but from external sources as well—a business can evolve to move beyond operational intelligence and automation to tactical and even strategic intelligence by hypothesizing, answering and acting upon various business scenarios.

If only a vision for many businesses today, it's one that's not too far down the road. Those that don't figure out how to become more of a self-driving business eventually will be driven into the ground.

101: MANUFACTURING MONEY FROM IMPROVED PRICING ANALYTICS

#usa #northamerica #transaction #reporting
#dataquality #erp #customer #manufacturing

Headquartered in Menomonee Falls, Wisconsin, Bradley Corporation is a leading fixture company that specializes in manufacturing washroom and accessories, and commercial plumbing fixtures. For decades, it has been providing quality service to a diverse customer base, from small local facilities to international corporations.

The company has been experiencing rapid growth in its business over the past 10 years; it kept on gaining new customers and adding new products to its portfolio. With the growth, the pricing models got too difficult to update and identify in the ERP system. Updating the price book and job quotes required multiple spreadsheets and tribal knowledge, which consumes time and money, and is error-prone.

They developed pricing yield management toolsets and processes that utilized the company's transaction data to create a comprehensive management report that can be used to identify areas to increase pricing across customers, products, and regions. Furthermore, they hypothesized that there were potential opportunities to utilize management reporting tools to provide sales yield transparency across the enterprise, which in turn, would probably result in an increased upper extreme of the operating income.

They also established pricing baselines and set goals for every product line and customer. KPIs and "continuous improvement" processes were also introduced to monitor the company's progress now and then. The yield management toolset and process analyze Bradley's transaction data to create a collection of comprehensive management reports to identify if a price increase is feasible in a particular region, product, and customer group. Moreover, the tool is capable of generating sales reports, which can be used to assess and improve sales in under-marketed product groups.

Bradley was able to instantly realize price increases in the market and quickly realize price fluctuations in the market, focusing more on the price increase and cash rather than deeper discounts. This resulted in increased operating income considering the same type of product, volume of product, and customers to whom the products were sold.

In the first year of implementation, Bradley already experienced positive changes in its sales. After augmenting data quality, using analytics to identify the most effective pricing of products, and training sales representatives, the company realized a sales price improvement of 4% in Q1, 4.6% in Q2, 6.2% in Q3, and 6.3% in Q4. In the second year, Bradley was able to realize an additional $8M in its operating income and gained an increase in its gross YOY sales to existing customers by analyzing customer data from Share of Wallet and salesperson product mix and through the discovery of a $300K recurring pricing error in its old system.

Expert Analysis by Lisa C. Palmer

Chief Technical Adviser, Americas, Splunk, and 2021 Who's Who in AI

Bradley Corporation exhibited common markers of organizations fraught with pricing challenges. Created by rapid growth, widely varying customer profiles, and an onslaught of new products, complexity and desperation drove staff and leaders to create manual processes outside of their core system. This reactivity to short-term needs kept the organization functioning, but lowered profitability and caused errors that were likely frustrating employees and negatively impacting customer satisfaction. Sadly, business situations just like this exist all around the world.

As is often the case when leaders shift focus to longer-term strategic thinking, data fueled Bradley's destiny. Analytics allowed them to gain control over their situation.

Understanding how pricing activities affected their overall business, analyzing the profitability of different price points, quickly pivoting pricing when market conditions shifted, and optimizing pricing strategy for maximum revenue were all accomplished with pricing analytics. Undoubtedly, they faced internal organizational and personnel resistance as needs for new governance, process changes, and systems adjustments became apparent. Externally, they faced partner and customer acceptance issues.

Throughout such a massive change management effort, it is powerful to reference the same hard data that informed leadership's choices. Regardless of your role, data is compelling!

Bradley's operating income results quickly proved the tangible value of decisions based upon hard data. Although some of these results were from "quick wins" such as identifying errors and obvious customer cross-selling, many sustained opportunities exist. Enriching existing analytics with continually updated and added datasets, both internal and external, will allow for next level insights and actions. Actions enabled could include optimizing products and pricing for each customer segment and against specific competitors, aligning sales compensation plans to drive profit growth, and quick identification/remediation of customer satisfaction issues to enable retention. Bottom line, Bradley is off to a great start with rich opportunities on their horizon!

About the Author

Doug Laney is a best-selling author and recognized authority on data and analytics strategy. He advises senior IT, business and data leaders on data monetization and valuation, data management and governance, external data strategies, analytics best practices, and establishing data and analytics organizations.

Doug's book, *Infonomics: How to Monetize, Manage, and Measure Information for Competitive Advantage,* was selected by CIO Magazine as the "Must-Read Book of the Year" and a "Top 5 Books for Business Leaders and Tech Innovators."

Now the Data & Analytics Strategy Innovation Fellow with the digital services consulting firm West Monroe, previously Doug was a founding member and Distinguished Analyst with Gartner's Chief Data Officer research and advisory team, and is a three-time Gartner annual thought leadership award recipient. In addition, he helped launch and co-manage the Deloitte Analytics Institute, is a Forbes contributing writer and has been published in the Wall Street Journal and the Financial Times among other journals.

Doug guest-lectures at major business schools around the world and is a visiting professor with the University of Illinois Gies College of Business where he teaches an MBA course on Infonomics and developed its Business Analytics Executive Overview course, both of which are available online via Coursera.

Doug also co-chairs the annual MIT CDO/IQ Symposium, is a visiting professor at Carnegie Mellon University's Heinz College, is a member of the World Economic Forum's data exchange initiative, a member of the American Economic Association, on the Dataversity and TDWI faculty, and sits on various technology company advisory boards.

In his "spare time" Doug enjoys cycling the Chicago lakefront, golfing, Cubs games, cooking and hosting dinner parties, chilling on his rooftop deck, good wine and great whiskey, reading and podcasts, and volunteering at the Lakeview Pantry and teaching Junior Achievement classes at grammar schools.

INDEX